HALLELUJAH, ANYHOW!

HALLELUJAH, ANYHOW!

A Memoir

Barbara C. Harris

With Kelly Brown Douglas

CHURCH
PUBLISHING
INCORPORATED

Unless otherwise noted, the Scripture quotations contained herein are from the New Revised Standard Version Bible, copyright © 1989 by the Division of Christian Education of the National Council of Churches of Christ in the U.S.A. Used by permission. All rights reserved.

Church Publishing
19 East 34th Street
New York, NY 10016
www.churchpublishing.org

Cover photo: Portrait of Bishop Barbara Harris by Timothy Greenfield-Sanders

Cover design by Marc Whitaker, MTWdesign
Typeset by Rose Design

Library of Congress Cataloging-in-Publication Data

A record of this book is available from the Library of Congress.

ISBN-13: 978-1-64065-089-3 (pbk.)
ISBN-13: 978-1-64065-090-9 (ebook)

Printed in the United States of America

Dedication

For Dorothy, Millicent (now deceased), and Marilyn:
my dearest friends for more than 70 years
and for my late sister Joey (Josephine Harris White)
my biggest cheerleader.

CONTENTS

ACKNOWLEDGMENTS

The Rev. John Ferris Smith, former chaplain at Groton School, Groton, Massachusetts, got me started on this project in a different narrative format many years ago.

The Rev. Dr. Kelly Brown Douglas prodded me to resume the work and is responsible for ably helping me to bring it to completion.

With thanks to the Rev. Canon Edward Rodman and the Rev. Canon Nan A. Peete for their gracious foreword and afterword, respectively.

FOREWORD

Some forty-nine years ago I first met Barbara Harris at the formational meeting of the Black Clergy and Laity Organization held at Saint Augustine's College in Raleigh, North Carolina in 1968. The Union of Black Clergy and Laity would become the Union of Black Episcopalians. From that day until this I have been privileged to witness and sometimes participate in the epic story of her emergence as the first female bishop in the Anglican Communion and an unparalleled leader of women and men. As you delve into this remarkable woman's life you will be ably guided by the inspired choice of the Rev. Dr. Kelly Brown Douglas, a noted Episcopal priest and scholar in her own right, through her insightful and probing questions of Barbara; their dialogue ensues with pace and clarity. In the annals of memoirs this motif may emerge as a preferred model for allowing the story of Barbara's life to unfold without embellishment or self-serving apologetics.

I would not attempt to add my own personal perspective because I in no way want to distract from the power of the story as it unfolds in this dialogic manner. I will only share two brief stories about my interaction with Barbara that are reflective of Barbara's humor and grace. On the steps of the Cathedral of Saint Paul in Boston, immediately following that memorable initial press conference that introduced Barbara to the world, a pigeon flew overhead and made a deposit on her immaculately coiffed afro. As she paused to get over the shock and run through the possible emotions she might have legitimately had, she finally chuckled and said in her typical self-deprecating fashion, "I guess God is trying to keep me in my place." Not only was this a humorous and humbling moment, it was authentically prophetic as it prepared her for many decidedly less humorous shots that were taken at her as she trod the treacherous path from consecration to retirement.

The other story is reflective of Barbara's remarkable compassion and unique relationship that developed between her and Bishop Thomas Shaw, following the suicide of his predecessor Bishop David Johnson. At the close of the Philadelphia General Convention in 1998, Bishop Shaw approached me and inquired if I drove to the convention from Boston. It was a curious question but when he asked if I was bringing Barbara back as well, my cynical curiosity was peaked, especially since my assistant Ann Marie Marvel, Barbara, and I were all smokers, a habit which he detested. It did not take long for him to reveal his purpose—in a six hour drive back to Foxboro, he cunningly and deftly convinced her to stay in the diocese for three more years while he sought to raise the money and the enthusiasm to create the Barbara C. Harris Camp and Conference Center. This was a well-conceived and brilliant idea which he was able to convince her to do, despite her many efforts to talk him out of it. Needless to say, I have never let Barbara forget this episode of grace and gullibility. For such a worldly woman who has seen much and endured more, it was a sight to remember.

As I close this foreword I invite you to enjoy, learn from, and gain insight into the life and practice of my good friend and sister Barbara C. Harris.

It is well worth it and you will gain a deeper appreciation of the constant refrain that punctuates every remarkable story, "hallelujah, anyhow."

Edward W. Rodman

Hallelujah anyhow
Never let your troubles get you down
Whenever troubles come your way
Hold your hands up high and say
Hallelujah anyhow!

—words and music by Joseph Pace

PREFACE

Why the title? The hymn "Hallelujah Anyhow" is reflective of the attitude I have attempted to carry through life, or at least my adult life. It speaks in a real way to the ups and downs, the peaks and valleys, and the sure knowledge that whatever happens along life's rugged pathway, "it is well with my soul."

Hymns permeate my life. They are for me a form of prayer or an entry into prayer. From my earliest days in Sunday school the hymns were the best part of church for me. I am often teased because I seldom open a hymn book. I know so many by heart: all the verses and quite a few of the page numbers of the Episcopal Church's 1940 *Hymnal*—my preference over the 1982 version, by the way. The same is true for the old *Baptist Standard Hymnal*, *The New National Baptist Hymnal*, that little gem, *Gospel Pearls*—on which I almost cut my teeth as my neighbor, Baptist deacon "Pop" Houston and I used to leaf through from start to finish, sitting on his front porch; *Songs of Zion* (a United Methodist supplemental worship resource which was edited by a childhood neighbor, Dr. Verologa Nix), *Lead Me, Guide Me* (the African American Catholic Hymnal), and *Lift Every Voice I* and *II* (both Episcopal hymn book supplements in the black and gospel music idiom).

Back in Sunday school at St. Barnabas Church in the Germantown section of Philadelphia, where I grew up, Miss Evelyn Jones—who did not have the best singing voice in town, but a heart full of love for little children—taught us songs I still remember almost in their entirety. There were children's hymns such as the one that went "Jesus tender shepherd hear me, bless thy little lamb tonight. Through the darkness, be Thou near me, keep me safe 'til morning light," and "There's a friend for little children above the bright blue sky . . ." And every Sunday, as we reluctantly gave up our pennies to that mysterious brass offering plate, we sang "Savior bless thy truths we pray, help us live them day by day, in them live, in them love, teach us from above."

I enter my prayer closet each day with a hymn on my heart and often on my lips. My night prayer ends with a hymn—usually the first one I was given to learn by my Episcopal piano teacher, Kate Waring Taylor—"The day thou gavest Lord is ended, the darkness falls at thy behest. To thee our morning hymns ascended, thy praise shall sanctify our rest."

I also remember the closing hymn at my service of confirmation on a bitter cold Monday night, December 11, 1941—somehow our aging white bishop, who wore white cotton gloves when he visited Black congregations so that he did not ever have to touch our heads, never seemed to get around to us on Sundays. Nevertheless, I was struck by the words, "Go forward Christian soldier, beneath his banner true. The Lord himself thy leader, will all thy foes subdue. His love foretells thy trials, He knows thine hourly need. He will with bread of heaven, thy fainting spirit feed." At age eleven I thought nothing could harm me and I felt completely invincible. With such a promise ringing in my little ears, how could it be otherwise? Well, the years have told a different tale, but hey—Hallelujah anyhow!

Few of my sermons are concluded without a line or two or a verse from some old hymn which poetically sums up scripture references or a thought I am trying to express. Many people come to expect it, and I tend to believe that some would be disappointed if I didn't follow the practice—if only for a laugh. Moreover, my conversations frequently get a hymn thrown in.

Since I am writing this, it would be easy and oh so tempting to paint myself as a "child sacristy rat" who grew into a kind of plaster saint or a still living, breathing martyr. Let's face it, the most favorable thing that will probably be written about my life is my episcopate and my experience as a bishop, but in all honesty I have to own my warts and 'fess up to the fact that "I have left undone those things which I ought to have done and I have done those things that I ought not to have done." Somehow I always choked on the next line of that confession and found it hard to acknowledge that there was "no health" in me.

Realizing that some who may chance to read this volume are not Episcopalians, I have sprinkled the text with explanations of some things about the church, its governance, canons and customs, for which I hope my Episcopal brothers and sisters will indulge me and endure.

> Well, here goes: Hallelujah, anyhow!
> Barbara C. Harris

INTRODUCTION

[Text in Kelly Brown Douglas's voice throughout the book will be inset and in this font. The words of Bishop Harris will be set with standard margins and a serif font.]

I love to tell the story
Of unseen things above,
Of Jesus and His glory,
Of Jesus and his love.
I love to tell the story,
Because I know its true;
It satisfies my longings
As nothing else would do.
I love to tell the story,
'Twill be my theme in glory
To tell the old, old story
Of Jesus and His love.

—Kate Hankey and William G. Fischer

Douglas: *Why is this book important to you?*

Harris: *I want people to know the real Barbara.*

This book project started as a memoir. Bishop Harris had begun the writing but with the demands of life and the passing of time her writing slowed. However, even as the writing slowed, her passion for completing this book grew. She wanted people to know her story. She wanted people to know the woman underneath the miter and behind the cope. She invited me to join her in trying to bring this book project to completion. I was humbled and daunted by the invitation but gladly accepted it. I had thought for some time that hers was a story that needed to be told. Over the years of knowing the bishop, I learned so much from being in her presence.

From the first time I met her she took me in. It was a Sunday afternoon at the Church of the Intercession in New York City. She had been recently ordained to the priesthood. I was a seminarian. She was the first black female priest that I ever met; in fact she was the first female priest I had encountered. I was excited at the same time that I was very nervous in anticipation of meeting her. The woman I met that day exceeded whatever expectations I had. I was immediately struck by her small stature yet powerful presence; I was awestruck by her very dignified humility. As I stood shyly in the corner of the sacristy—trying not to be noticed—she approached me and asked me who I was and what I was doing at Intercession. I nervously responded to her questions, trying to say enough, but not talk too much. I couldn't imagine that she was doing anything other than being polite and that whatever I told her would fall out of memory no sooner than she left my company. However, when I shared with her who I was, where I was in the ordination process (at the time a postulant), she listened intently. Clearly, her question was more than simply a courtesy; she really wanted to know. She said she was going to keep in touch and that I should call her if I needed anything. She offered her support to me not because I was special, but because she was special. What I came to realize was that my initial encounter with her was not unique. It reflected her very ministry.

Hers has been a ministry defined by paving the way for others, especially young black women, to claim their call in the church and their voice in the world. In fact, it was she who paved the way for Gayle Harris to succeed her as suffragan bishop of Massachusetts. Moreover, as I have gotten to know Bishop Harris, I have learned that one of her greatest frustrations is the lack of support that female clergy show to one another, particularly when it is just a matter of showing up, of being present. The Barbara Harris I know always shows up. The road she walks, she walks for others. And so it was with humility that I agreed to help her with this project. It was my way of giving back in some small way to the woman that has given so much to me and others. It was my way of showing up.

The plan was for me to interview her so that I could fill in the gaps and continue to write her story in typical memoir form. However, as I was transcribing the interviews, one thing became clear: Barbara's story was best told by Barbara—in her own words, in her own voice. It doesn't take long when one is in Barbara's company to realize that she is a consummate storyteller. Therefore, I wanted this book to capture the powerful storyteller that is Barbara. I wanted to maintain the rhythm of her memory and the honesty of her words. The best way to do this was to weave the interviews into her written narratives, while maintaining the integrity of the actual interviews.

Indeed, the interviews proved as reflective of Barbara's personality and spirit as her written words. To edit them in any way, in an effort to integrate them into the narrative in a seamless memoir-like fashion, would be to deprive the reader of experiencing the charisma, the wit, and the sheer energy of this woman. I wanted the reader to get to know the person that I knew. I wanted the reader to feel as if they were in conversation with Barbara at the same time that they were sharing her memories. I wanted the reader to have as much of a first person, unmediated experience with Barbara as possible. It is for these reasons that I let Barbara's spoken words stand as they were, using them to illuminate or add to the story she had already written. In this way the reader is able to be in conversation with Barbara at the same time that they are sharing in the stories behind the conversation.

What follows is Barbara telling her story. Any gaps in how the story is told are the fault of the interviewer not the storyteller. Nonetheless, to listen and to read the words of Barbara is to be invited into a journey of an ordinary woman who has paved an extraordinary path. Through the years, Barbara would often remind me that God uses the weak to confound the strong. It is my hope that after reading this book the reader will have no doubt that God has indeed used this small vessel of a black woman to confound the strong powers of a church, if not the world. In these pages of conversation and storytelling, the reader will meet a woman who has answered the call of God to be a glimpse of God's very presence in the world, thereby opening a space for others who look like her to respond to God's call to them.

Kelly Brown Douglas

Early Times

Fire Shut up in my bones
Like Jeremiah, it won't leave me alone
Gonna sing 'til the almighty power comes around
Spirit's got me so I can't sit down

—Perry Stone

CHAPTER ONE

A Cloud of Witnesses

I t was a Saturday morning in Boston. I was in the front row of the balcony, the perfect seat for seeing all that was about to unfold on the floor of the auditorium beneath me. As Barbara came into view in the midst of this mighty procession of Episcopal authority, what struck me was the simultaneous smallness and command of the woman who was the center of attention that day. She walked down the aisle with a bearing of poised self-possession as she swayed to the rhythms of the music. When she approached the front of the auditorium to take her seat in the first row, I wondered what was going through her mind. I wondered about whom she was thinking. Who, I wondered, was walking down that aisle with her—who was in the cloud of witnesses, past and present, who brought her to that moment and were still keeping watch over her? In this chapter Barbara tells the stories of those great witnesses in her life. It is a story primarily of strong women that begins and ends with her mother.

This cloud of witnesses gave to Barbara a profound knowledge of how to thrive with dignity in a world that would despise her for her race and her gender. This was not a knowledge cultivated in a classroom and handed down in a dispassionate professorial voice. Rather, this was the "every-day taken for granted knowledge born from the experiences and hardships of living."[1] It was therefore knowledge handed

---

1. Patricia Hill Collins, *Black Feminist Thought: Knowledge, Consciousness and the Politics of Empowerment* (New York: Routledge 2000), 36.

down in such a manner to reflect the fierce determination of black women trying to make do and do better for themselves and their children in, as Audre Lorde describes, "the mouth of a racist, sexist suicidal dragon. . . ."[2]

It was this cloud of witnesses that carried Barbara into Hynes Auditorium that Saturday morning, with one in particular leading the way: her mother Beatrice P. Harris.

Over the years that I have known Barbara, there is probably no woman that I have heard her reference or speak about more than her mother. Her mother, who died in 1993 at age ninety-one, clearly remains a major influence in Barbara's life—not simply because of the values and knowledge she imparted, or the fact that she raised Barbara and her siblings in the church, but because she was a strong, determined woman who would not be "pushed around" (like mother, like daughter). While I never met Barbara's mother in person, Barbara's memory of her brings her to life, letting you know how truly Barbara is her mother's daughter. It is no wonder she was on Barbara's mind as she walked down the aisle toward her consecration. She feared the unsolicited "taken for granted wisdom" her mother might be moved to share that day. This chapter tells the story of her mother and the other cloud of witnesses that brought Barbara to that day.

The Women behind the Woman

"Yeah, and my mother always wanted the best for my siblings and me."

As the service opened I was almost dazzled by the spectacle, the eight thousand five hundred people gathered in the auditorium of Hynes Convention Center in Boston, the rows of bishops, sixty-two of them, the hundreds of clergy from all over the

---

2. Audre Lorde, "Man Child," in *Sister Outsider: Essays and Speeches* (Toronto: Crossing Press Feminist Series, 2007), 74.S

world, men and women. It seemed as if it was an endless line. And then there were the many friends and family from Philadelphia and beyond who gathered to share this moment with me. There was glorious music, brass fanfares, choirs from churches large and small, young people and old. I sat, as is custom, in the midst of the congregation of the people who had elected me bishop suffragan of Massachusetts. At the right moment, and in response to their call expressed through the presiding bishop of the Episcopal Church, Edmund Lee Browning, I would rise and accept responsibility and authority for all in whose midst I now sat.

As I sat there that day at the Hynes Auditorium amidst the panoply not only of a great ecclesiastical occasion but also the pressure and confusion of a major media event, I was also dreading what was to come. I knew that Bishop Browning, as the presiding bishop and chief consecrator that day, intended to allow those who objected to my ordination to voice their opposition in the midst of the service. The Book of Common Prayer provides such an opportunity, much as in a marriage ceremony. So in the least, I was nervous sitting there. But I began to worry even more about something other than the possible objections that would surely be voiced: the woman sitting across from me.

My mother was perched on her chair regarding one of the objectors with a piercing stare. Mom was not a woman who agreed particularly with St. Paul's admonition that we should "suffer fools gladly," and she was then of an age when she figured she could do and say anything she wanted. I knew that if she started to tap her foot and narrow her lips we could expect a strong response to what was going on. I could picture her approaching the man at the microphone and asking in front of that huge crowd with all those cameras trained on her, "Now just what is your problem?"

My mother was an only girl; she had four brothers and she was spoiled too. Mom had a sense of entitlement and a firm sense of herself always. From time to time she did domestic work, but she did it elegantly, which is how she did everything, even when she took in washing and ironing to pay for my piano and voice lessons. She used to sip on a little bourbon while she ironed because she said the steam got in her throat.

Sparing details, I will only say that I reached a point in my adult life when I refused to sit next to my mother at family obsequies because her wry side-of-the-mouth comments reduced me to tears of laughter while she sat straight-faced and seemingly absorbed in or focused on the rituals of the deceased. Which reminds me of my father's mother's burial.

Our cortege was held up in the cemetery while another family completed an interment. My mother got out of the car and suddenly seemed to collapse against the door of the limousine in which we were riding. We had to climb out the other side of the car to determine the nature of her distress and with tears (of laughter) in her eyes she pointed to the ground. There in the snow in the cemetery lay an obviously used condom. Mom said, "I guess the spirits have sex out here."

Douglas: *Is there any story, any event, any interaction that most reflects you and your mother's relationship and her influence on you and who you are?*

Harris: *My mother was a trained musician, and I loved music, and my mother sacrificed so that I could have music lessons: piano and voice. And (long pause) well, there was a period when she was church organist and I was in the choir as she was organist and choir director, but, as a teenager, or pre-teen and teenager, my mother took in laundry, washing and ironing, to pay for my music lessons—so that it didn't come out of the household budget, this was an extra responsibility that she took on so that I could have this, I won't call it a luxury, so that I could have this opportunity and this privilege. And, I was deeply grateful for that because I knew that that was hard for her to do. She didn't earn a lot of money doing it but enough to cover the costs of my weekly piano lessons and my lessons as part of a vocal group.*

(Long pause). So, from early on, I had my mother's support for good things in life. Yeah, and my mother always wanted the best for my siblings and me.

Douglas: *Was there a time when you truly defied your mother's wishes for you, even knowing that she wanted the best for you?*

Harris: *Yes, my wedding day when we pulled up to the church and my mother said "Are you sure you want to do this?" and I said, "What do you mean?" and she said, "Because we can pull around the corner and go on back home and it'll all be over."*

Douglas: *Your mother didn't want you to get married?*

Harris: *Not really.*

Douglas: *Why didn't you listen to her?*

Harris: *Because I didn't think my mother, I was thirty years old, and I didn't think my mother needed to judge my choice of a marriage partner. I suppose she wanted what she thought was the best for me in a marriage partner and, um, this person was not "it" in her opinion. I had to practically bribe her to get her to come to the wedding. I resented her being so vocal in her objection.*

Douglas: *And did that make you become even more headstrong about wanting to do it?*

Harris: *Not in the sense of trying to win a battle over her, but I thought I knew what I was doing and I was just determined that I was going to do, in this instance, what I wanted to do.*

Douglas: *And, what about your ordination? What did your mother think about that?*

Harris: *My mother was not very supportive of the ordination of women and particularly of mine, but I guess . . . I don't know what her objections were because she had had no real experience of ordained women. But I think her reaction to my seeking ordination was that not just a general objection or reluctance to* *accept ordination of women but that she probably felt that I was not a worthy candidate.*

Douglas: *And why's that?*

Harris: *I guess she just never saw her daughter as a likely person to be ordained. Her model for ordained ministry came way, way out of the past with a rigid, stern, but loving priest—under whom she and we had all grown up. So, I was nowhere near her image or her model of ordained ministry. And I guess knowing all my flaws and shortcomings, she could not imagine the church approving her flawed daughter in the ranks of its ordained clergy. I guess it was kind of, "Well if you knew what I knew about her, you wouldn't want her either."*

In the end, my mother came around to my ordination, at least partially evidenced by the fact of the numbers of her friends who showed up for my ordination as a deacon. In fact, by the time I was ordained priest she was actually one of my strongest supporters. When someone wondered aloud if more people had attended my ordination or that of another woman my mother interrupted in classic motherly fashion saying: "It doesn't make any difference. Barbara had four bishops at her ordination!"

Womanist Roots

"I don't need anybody to fight for me. I can fight for myself and I'm not a little boy."

As I listened to Barbara talk about her mother all I could think of was Alice Walker's definition of "womanist."[3] In this four-part definition, Walker tells us that a womanist is outrageous, audacious, courageous and prone to willful behavior. Barbara's womanist character has been evident throughout her journey, and there was little doubt where it came from. However, the "womanist" DNA ran deep in Barbara. To search Barbara's

---

3. Alice Walker, *In Search of Our Mothers' Gardens: Womanist Prose*, reprint ed. (New York: Mariner Books, 2003).

womanist DNA is to discover other women in her life who were just as outrageous, audacious, courageous and willful. These were women that I had never heard Barbara speak of, but a mutual friend of ours, the Rev. Nan Peete, told me that there were amazing women in Barbara's life; I should be sure to ask her about them. And so I did.

Douglas: *Now clearly, you get that, what then they called feistiness, from your mother. Were all the women of your family so feisty or what we might call today "womanish?"*

Harris: *I think some of my feistiness comes from my great-grandmother. She had been a slave on the Brauner plantation in Maryland. We called her Mom Sem, Sem was the short version of her married name, Sembley. She used to tell the wonderful story about her encounter on the plantation with General Grant. He came onto the plantation one day and asked her for a drink of water. So she pumped a dipper for him. He rinsed it out, threw it aside, and asked her to pump another. She said, "You didn't need to rinse that out. It was clean." He replied, "People around her have been trying to poison people like us. I've been South fighting for little boys like you." My great-grandmother wore her hair close-cropped, even more so than I do mine, so she said to Grant, "I don't need anybody to fight for me. I can fight for myself and I'm not a little boy." I think she was about twelve years old.*

Douglas: *Now she told you that story or was it handed down?*

Harris: *I don't know how, whether she told me directly, I think she told me that directly but she was feisty because immediately following Emancipation, she changed her name from Adelaide Eliza Brauner to Ida Brauner. She had a twin sister who was sold South and while I do not know the details of it, miraculously, they were reunited in Washington, DC, after Emancipation. I wish I knew the details of the story, but I don't. I only know that they were reunited. She lived in DC until the family moved to Philadelphia.*

Douglas: *Are there any other stories, or recollections that you have, that she told you about her days as a slave?*

Harris: *No, that's all I know about her days as a slave, but I do know what kind of personality she was. If she liked you, there was nothing she wouldn't do for you. And if she did not like you, there was nothing she would do for you. She approved of my sister and took my sister into her room, closed the door, and taught my sister to sew. The door was shut in my face and she told me, "Thee is not fit for human company," and I was not allowed into the room. I remember lying on my stomach in the hall pushing buttons under door and saying, "Postman! Special Delivery!" One day when I was doing that, my grandmother, her oldest daughter, came tiptoeing up the stairs and the next thing I knew there a wire coat hanger across my backside. That was the last time I played Postman.*

Douglas: *There was a time in the black community that grand-mothers and especially great-grandmothers were treated as respected matriarchs. Was this the way it was for Mom Sem?*

Harris: *My great-grandmother was very regal. I can remember her taking me to the store with her and she would walk very erect down the street and I could not, at age seven or eight, under-stand why she was carrying a huge black umbrella in the mid-dle of a sunny August day. I didn't realize then she was shading herself from the sun. I was just embarrassed because I thought it looked so ridiculous to be walking the street in a bright August sunshine with a huge black man's umbrella over her head. But, as we passed the corner saloon, the men all standing outside all removed their hats and nodded and said, "Good afternoon, Ms. Sembley." So, she had a lot of respect in the neighborhood.*

Douglas: *So, you clearly spent a lot of time with your great-grandmother.*

Harris: *She lived with us until I was eight years old; she died in 1938. When my great-grandmother died I remember that I was* *playing around the corner with a cousin and my sister—who was five years older than me and who died in 2006, three days before her eighty-first birthday—came running and said, "You kids come on home. Mom Sem just died." Of course, death didn't have any meaning for me and in those days children didn't go to funerals. The undertaker came and carried her body out in a wicker basket, but it still didn't register. She was gone, that's all; we never saw her again.*

Douglas: *So what do you think she would have thought of your ordination to the priesthood and your subsequent consecration as bishop?*

Harris: *I don't think she could have even conceived of it.*

A word about my grandmother, Mom Sem's daughter Mary Matile Sembley Price. I once shared this in a homily. I learned much from my grandmother for whom the daily round was sweeping floors and dusting and cleaning other people's houses. When most had finished an eight-hour day, she went on to yet another job of cleaning up behind dirty adolescent boys at a private day school—emptying wastebaskets, mopping floors, and readying the untidy headmaster's office for the next day I joined her on Friday afternoons for "grand rounds" of washing blackboards and dusting fifty-four captain's chairs in the study hall—legs and all—for which she shared with me from her meager wages the grand sum of fifty cents per week. And God knows I hated every minute and every penny of it. She walked home in the dark every night and I alongside her on Friday evenings, singing hymns or breathing out little one-line prayers such as "Lord, if I just can make it to my Father's house," or "Jesus, God from glory, come down here." Sometimes it was "I thank you, Jesus and I thank you, Lord." I shared this on the day the church commemorates the life of George Herbert, priest, poet, and writer of prose. It also is my grandmother's birth date. Some of Herbert's poems have been set to music and have found their way into the hymns of the church.

My grandmother's prayers hardly match his poetry or prose, but they were no less sincere. One of his poems found in our 1982 hymnal sums up for me my grandmother's life and I asked the small group to which I was speaking to sing it for all the little Mattie Prices of this world whose humble lives were lived to God's praise and God's glory. The hymn goes like this: "Teach me my God and King, in all things thee to see, and what I do in anything, to do it as for thee."

A Sister/Friend

"I'm your older sister. I'm allowed to hit you."

Douglas: *Tell me more about your sister. Was she as feisty as you or the other women in your family?*

Harris: *My sister, Joey, as I said, was five years older than me. She was more docile. My sister was very quiet and not very ambitious, but a little bossy. She hit me once and I hit her back. She said to me, "How dare you!" and I said, "You hit me." She came back, "I'm your older sister. I'm allowed to hit you." For a long time my sister convinced me that I was adopted and had been left on the doorstep. She said mom and daddy felt sorry for me because I had such awful hair so they took me in. One day I got up the courage to ask my mother if I'd been adopted. She said, "Where'd you ever get that notion," and I said "Joey told me." That was the first time I saw my nice, nice sister get a whipping. It was sheer delight.*

My sister was an unusual person. She never sought anything for herself but gave herself over to nurturing the whole family. She was always content to bask in any success I enjoyed. She was my strongest supporter and a wonderful friend. She said once, "My sister did not have to be elected by the Diocese of Massachusetts for me to know she's the greatest person on earth." How's that for fierce support?

The Other Side

"Oh, Grandma!"

Douglas: *All of those about whom you speak are on your maternal side; what about your paternal side of the family?*

Harris: *My father's family, which emanated in Richmond, Virginia, was constituted much the same as my mother's. Daddy also was one of four brothers with one sister. Because we lived with my maternal grandparents, I saw more of them than my father's mother and other members of that branch of the family. There was a slavery history on my father's side of the family as well. His grandmother, Rosa Funn, was a house slave, a seamstress. Before leaving for a trip to Europe, her owners told her that if she was a "good girl" she could get married on their return. Her wedding ring, a delicate band set with three pearls, became my mother's engagement ring. My mother allowed my sister to "dress up" with it from time to time and eventually it was passed to me because pearls are my birthstone.*

Douglas: *What were the women like on your father's side of the family? What kind of relationship did you have with them?*

Harris: *Not a very strong one.*

Douglas: *Say more.*

Harris: *My grandmother Harris was a very fair-skinned woman, whom most people, including myself had I not known her, would have assumed was white. In fact, one afternoon I was coming from a piano lesson and I got on the streetcar and sat down next to my father's mother and I did not speak to her because I didn't look at her, I just thought I was sitting next to some white woman that I didn't know. She let me ride four blocks and she said, "Good afternoon, miss." Scared me to death. And I turned and said, "Oh, Grandma!" You can believe I studied the faces of petite white women with a lot more care after that.*

Douglas: *You're kidding!*

Harris: *And she was on her way to my house to meet with my maternal grandmother about some organization to which they both belonged. And I was scared to death about what she was going to say.*

One undeniable aspect of slavery is reflected in skin complexion. The fact that slave women had children with slave masters showed up in many fair-skinned African Americans of former generations. And so it was with members of my father's family. One of my father's early jobs was acquired because his employer mistook him for a white person. It was when Daddy refused to buy tickets for a Polish dance and gave his reason, "I'm not Polish, I'm colored," that he lost the job in matter of hours.

Gentle Men

"If nothin's what you ask for, nothin's what you get."

> While the women in Barbara's life perhaps had the most influence in shaping her personality, and perhaps were God's hands in making her "fit" to take the hits that would come with being the first woman bishop in the Anglican Communion, the men in her life were no less influential. For to know Barbara—even in all of her womanish feistiness—is to know a gentle spirit and soul that cares deeply for the most vulnerable in our world, one who is as kind in spirit as she is fierce in words. When one hears about the men in Barbara's life, one quickly recognizes where this gentle spirit comes from. It is fitting then that Barbara would be the one to overturn the gendered expectations of a bishop in the Anglican Communion, as in fact those expectations were overturned within her own family. The women in her family were not the demure females that women were expected to be and the men were not the domineering figures that a patriarchal model of gender roles demanded of them.

My grandfather was a delight. He ran a crab house which was really a front for a gambling joint. He served deviled crabs and hard-shell crabs, but the real action was in the back room. He had a shiny sign up which said, "Jesus Never Fails," which must have been a great consolation to the gamblers. Grandpop taught us to tap dance, to do the Buck n' Wing and the Charleston. He fiddled around on the piano, playing songs with strange names like "Big Bertha," and "Thompson Street." I doubt whether the words would be appropriate if printed here. He called us his "gandsies" and invented great games the whole family could join in playing.

He did teach me some valuable lessons. For example, he always said you should ask for more than you want. Once I asked him for a penny and that was all I got. "Grandpop, is that all you're going to give me?" I asked, and he responded, "If you wanted a nickel, you should have asked for a dime. If nothin's what you ask for, nothin's what you get."

Douglas: *One person you don't talk much about is your father. Tell me about him.*

Harris: *My father was a quiet, loving person but left all the disciplinary aspects of our growing up to my mother—except that if he was in disapproval of something, he would let you know, but the actual meting out of any discipline was kind of left to my mother. I remember announcing something that I wanted to do at age nineteen. He said he didn't think I should do it. I grandly announced that "I'm as much woman now as I'll ever be." He looked at me sadly and said, "If you're as much woman now as you'll ever be, then shame on you."*

My father was a very quiet, unassuming person who deeply loved us but did not have a very forceful role in the household and I suspect a part of that was because he was living under his mother-in-law and father-in-law's roof and so he was not the master of his own household. While I didn't understand it then, in retrospect, I suspect that had a lot to do with his quiet, unassuming attitude and behavior.

My father also taught me to play poker and I learned the hard way. At my insistent urging he agreed to explain the rudiments of the game, told me to put my money on the table and dealt me a hand. He took twenty dollars from me in a matter of minutes and smiling put it in his pocket. "Okay Daddy," I said, "you can give me my twenty back now." He replied, "You would not get it back in a real game, so let this be a lesson to you." He never did return my twenty bucks, nor did I ever play much poker.

Douglas: *When did he pass away? How old were you?*

Harris: *My father died after a series of heart attacks and strokes. He would have a slight stroke and then bounce back: I think there were eleven of them. He died when I was 29, my brother was eighteen and I remember my brother saying, "I've lost the best friend that I ever had." And that left my brother in a house-hold with four women so he promptly enlisted in the air force, which was probably the smartest thing he could do.*

By the time of my father's death, we had a new rector at our parish church. Our rector emeritus did what today we strongly urge clergy retired from a parish not to do. He acceded to my mother's request that he conduct and preach the funeral—a huge mistake on my mother's part. Dear old Father Thomas saw the huge crowd, got excited and preached not one, but two sermons that went on so long we barcly had time to get to the cemetery on a Saturday afternoon before the grave diggers left.

Douglas: *And what was the impact of his death on you?*

Harris: *(Long Pause) I was saddened by my father's death, but I did not feel that a very powerful influence on my life had been lost. And, um, the next year, I got married. While I was a little sorry that my father wasn't there to see me married, I did not have deep regret about that.*

Douglas: *Is there any particular reason that you didn't have deep regret about that? Was that because he wasn't a powerful influence in your life or was it because you didn't want him to know who you married?*

Harris: *I'm not sure he would have approved of the person I married, my mother certainly didn't, and I think he might have joined her in her sentiment but not perhaps as vocally as she expressed her objections.*

Douglas: *Tell me about your brother.*

Harris: *My brother is 11 years younger than I am, and as my brother came along later and as the first boy child in the entire family, he was pampered and spoiled, so that he didn't have to struggle for anything.*

Douglas: *Ok, so you were . . .*

Harris: *I was part of the spoiling, pampering process . . .*

Douglas: *Yeah, so you were sort of raising him, you grew up not so much as siblings . . .*

Harris: *My sister and I were truly big sisters and we contributed to this process of pampering this first male child in the family. We all doted on my brother. He turned out to be all right despite the fact that he was spoiled. He was a nice kid who developed into a fine man. Even though he is in his early seventies I still think of him as my little brother (as did Joey until her death), and in 2001 Joey and I took a twenty-six hour train ride to celebrate his milestone sixtieth birthday with him in Florida.*

My brother was born in 1941, the first boy in the family. I think for my father he was the first baby boy in the whole world. I remember my father bought an expensive crib for him but wasn't able to keep up the payments on it, so the salesman came to the house to pick it up. Can you imagine someone coming to repossess a crib? My grandmother was sitting on the front porch crocheting. The man said, "Mr. Harris didn't keep up the payments and I'm here to take it back." Muz, as we called my grandmother, said, "It's upstairs in the back bedroom. You go right on up and get it but when you do don't plan on coming past me with it. You just go right on out the

back window." Like the rich young ruler in the Bible, he turned
and went sadly away.

And then there were the endless cousins, Roman Catho-
lics on one side and Baptists on the other. There were Cath-
olics, male and female, whose saint's name was Mary. Mary
Catherine, Mary Priscilla, Mary Harriet, Mary Philip, Mary
Francis and Mary Mary, who was known as "Big Mary." The
Baptists were equally interestingly named. Four sisters, Lizzie,
Lisa, Lola and "Lunky," were pretty dramatic and could turn a
family death and funeral into a rather raucous and sometimes
amusing affair.

I had a favorite cousin who was a good cook. Stockton
would come some days and fix pancakes, which was a treat. One
day I managed to eat nine. Mother usually sat at the table with
me, she didn't let me eat alone. One day she was busy upstairs
and I slipped out and went down the street to the Sheltons, who
had eight children. I sent one of the girls, my friend Reba, to my
house to eat my lunch while I ate bologna sandwiches and drank
lemonade with the Sheltons. When my mother came down and
saw Reba eating my lunch she was furious. I, on the other hand,
was in seventh heaven because we never had bologna in our
house. Besides, anything my mother didn't like was not good
for you and she did not like bologna. Hallelujah anyhow!

CHAPTER TWO

Church Girl/School Girl

A s I was putting this book together I intended to reorder the material in this chapter, separating the discussion about church and school. However, as I read and learned more about Barbara, it was clear why she put these two experiences together. Besides her family, there were probably no other institutions that shaped Barbara more than her church and school, particularly her high school. While she certainly experienced the limitations of being a female in church, it was indeed the "black church" which provided the oasis for Barbara to face the humiliations of a world that counted both her color and femaleness against her. Through the stories that Barbara tells concerning her life in the church, we experience with her the importance of the black church in black lives.

The black church is not a singular monolithic institution. It is a vast grouping of churches which mirrors the complex richness of the black community itself. The black church is as diverse as the community is diverse. Therefore, they vary in terms of size, denominational affiliations, worshipping culture, and numerous other factors. Some, for instance, are within white denominational systems, like the Episcopal Church, while others are independent of them, like the African Methodist Episcopal Church. While black churches are typically identifiable by their membership, the blackness of black churches actually goes beyond the racial makeup of its congregation. The black identity of a church is a matter of history and sociopolitical commitment. The black church emerged as a fundamental part of black peoples' resistance to white racist tyranny, as it was born in the "hush harbors" of slavery. In this regard, it is black churches' distinct involvement in the black struggle for life and freedom that determines their blackness. Essentially, the blackness of black churches is inextricably linked to their identification with a particular history and a commitment for the overall welfare of black people's bodies and souls. That Barbara was able to be nurtured throughout her life in a church that lived into its black identity is apparent in the stories she tells, leaving little doubt in the role it played in her becoming bishop in the Anglican Communion. This chapter tells that story.

Being Black in the Episcopal Church

"It's enough to make me ask what's the opposite of 'Hallelujah.'"

I'm a third generation Episcopalian. There have been times over the years however when I have wondered why I remained in the Episcopal Church given the racism, sexism and some other "isms" that pervade the life of the church. The church was an extension of our home; there was never any question about being involved.

We attended St. Barnabas Church in Germantown, which is the section of Philadelphia in which we lived. It was a joy to grow up in the atmosphere of that parish. The rector, the Rev. E. Sydnor Thomas, was a gentleman of the old school from the West Indies who was truly the spiritual father of the congregation. A fine role model and a good teacher, he was an extraordinary priest who taught us a lot about the history of blacks in the church, including the early Coptic fathers who brought order out of the chaos of the council of Niacea in 325 CE. I have in my possession the now out-of-print 1922 *History of the Afro-American Group of the Episcopal Church* by the Rev. George Freeman Bragg Jr., distinguished rector of St. James First African Church Baltimore, which Father Thomas gave to my grandmother for Christmas in 1928. My mother passed it on to me as an Easter gift in 1974. It is a rich volume which details the struggle of blacks for recognition, respect, dignity and equality in this "church of the presidents." It's enough to make me ask what's the opposite of "Hallelujah."

Father Thomas served our parish for forty-nine and a half years. It was then, about 1957 or shortly after, that the church brought in a mandatory retirement age and the bishop would not let him stay on for an additional six months, which broke his heart. The bishop said, "If I do it for you, I'll have to do it for everybody," which was not true. Besides, how many people stay in a parish for fifty years? This was a totally unnecessary thing to do. My final five months as bishop after age seventy-two is recompense for Father Thomas.

Being Female and Episcopalian

"And I thought that I was a worthy candidate and I resented the fact that I could not be elected to the vestry."

We were part of everything in that church: junior choir, young people's fellowship, etc. It was just the normal thing to do, being involved there, and I loved it. In fact, the church had such an influence on me I considered entering a religious order, but at the time the only order which admitted black women, other than the austere Sisters of the Transfiguration in Glendale, Ohio was in Canada.

Also, by that time I'd gotten a taste of worldly living and decided that the religious life was not for me. I asked my rector if there was any work in the mission field that an untrained person could do and he told me that sometimes there would be some administrative tasks in a mission house, such as in Liberia, but that never came to fruition. That might have been the seed or germ of my vocation to ordained ministry; although at the time I wouldn't have recognized it as such because we never even imagined ordination as being something women could, should, or would do.

Douglas: *Did you believe as well that women should not pursue ordain ministry?*

Harris: *There was nothing, there was nothing in my childhood or early church life that would ever make me conceive of ordination of women and certainly I would never have envisioned myself as an ordained person, but . . .*

Douglas: *Did you ever have a desire to serve, like the boys at the altar?*

Harris: *Well, there was enough that I could do in the church and church school. I did, I did wish that girls could serve on the altar as acolytes but it didn't, you know, eat at me. It wasn't, it wasn't a really annoying desire of mine. I was active in the junior choir and in the youth group. I later became a church school teacher and the advisor to the youth group. I taught church school with my mother, and . . . so my life in the church as a young person was as full as it could be at that time and beyond an active or active lay roles in the church, I never envisioned anything for myself. Well it was just unthinkable! At that time.*

Douglas: *You know, many people, particularly men who eventually become priests, tell these stories and I remember in my own life, going home in the basement and taking the little pool cue and the pool stick and parading around the pool table as if I were an acolyte because I couldn't do that in church. You don't have any of those play priest or acolyte moments in your childhood like that?*

Harris: *No, I have no childhood or teenage recollections of my playing into a role other than the roles in which I was serving as a member of the church school, the junior choir, and the JG, which was the junior guild, which we called the junior goons— and the things that I was already doing. I, I guess as I got into, I would say my early twenties, I found myself resentful that women in my parish could not serve on the vestry.*

Douglas: *Oh, you don't mention that in your manuscript So, they couldn't serve . . . women couldn't serve on the vestry?*

Harris: *No, according to the constitution of our parish, women could not . . . only men could serve on the vestry. And I found myself resenting that because the women were such strong supporters in the congregation, including the guild in which my mother served, which was one of the oldest acting guilds in the parish. It had been known as the Young Mother's Club, then the Mother's Club, and then it became the Matrons' Guild over time. And, plus, what was then known as the Women's Auxiliary which is the ECW at this point, these hardworking, loyal, and committed women, you might almost call them devout, were the strongest supporters of the congregation. They raised the money for things that needed to be done. If they saw a need, or if a need was spoken of, they quickly came to the fore and took it on as a labor of love. And I, I admired that but I was resentful that these women had no voice, or that women had no voice, in the governance of the parish or the congregation and a few years later when I was very active in the young adult's club, I led a little campaign in that group to see if we could legally have the charter, or I guess it was the charter of the church, changed so that women could serve on the vestry. And we offered to pay any court costs that might be entailed to make this come about.*

Douglas: *Now how do you leave that out of the manuscript, you're kidding!*

Harris: *I think it came to a head for me during one annual parish meeting when we were about to have elections for the vestry and rather than nominating any qualified women, it reached back. I looked in the back of the parish hall, and there sat a guy my age I knew and he hadn't been in church for at least eight or ten years and they had reached back and dragged him out to run for a seat on the vestry and I can remember being so furious! And I stood up in that parish meeting and I protested that active women were not being considered, could not be considered, for*

*the vestry. And the then rector was reluctant to take on the pres-
ent vestry to have the necessary documents changed, legally,
so that women could participate. He kinda went along to get
along on that particular issue. So we finally did get the charter,
I guess, and the constitution changed. And I remember the first
woman who was elected to the vestry, she would not have been
my choice but she served faithfully and well.*

Douglas: *What was her name? (Long Pause). That's ok if you
can't remember.*

Harris: *But I guess part of what was eating at me was that I
wanted to serve on the vestry myself. And I thought that I was
a worthy candidate and I resented the fact that I could not be
elected to the vestry.*

Douglas: *Yeah, because I was going to ask you what motivated
that and were you coming into a consciousness, a particular kind
of consciousness as a woman, perhaps a "feminist/womanist
consciousness" that motivated the protest?*

Harris: *I knew I was a qualified member of that congregation to
serve on its governing body and that got borne out for me years
later when I transferred my membership to the Church of the
Advocate, served on the vestry and was rector's senior warden
for a good ten years, if not more.*

Douglas: *Now tell me this, you were in your twenties when
you led this protest in your church, right, to get women onto
the vestry?*

Harris: *Yeah, I guess my mid-twenties.*

Douglas: *So, two things I want to ask about that. What did your
mother think of that, where was she on this issue? And two, did
it divide the church? But first what did your mother—was your
mother supportive of your move?*

Harris: *My mother, my mother thought that women should
be eligible for the vestry as well. I don't know that she was as*

vehement in her thought about it as I was, but she certainly felt that women should be eligible for the vestry, I don't think she had any desire herself to serve in that capacity but . . .

Douglas: *She didn't tell you, "Barbara, they should be, but tone it down"?*

Harris: *Oh no!*

Douglas: *So she supported her rebel daughter? (Laughter)*

Harris: *She was certainly sympathetic to the idea, if not as vehement about it as I was.*

Douglas: *Did it divide the church?*

Harris: *I don't think it really divided the church. Um, there were those of us in the young adult fellowship that felt very strongly about it, but we continued to support the church as we had, but when it came to a vote on whether or not women should be able to serve on the vestry, I would say that, that the majority of the members of the young adult fellowship were supportive of it, which is why, as I said, we agreed to assume any legal costs that might be incurred by the parish to make this change come about legally under the courts.*

Douglas: *In my young adult fellowship at St. Margaret's Church in Dayton, Ohio, we did bake sales and car washes to raise money, where did you all get money to even dare say that you were going to be able to assume legal costs?*

Harris: *We had fundraising events. I don't remember specifically, now, some of the things that we did, but we had a reasonable treasury and I think since we were working adults, that we would have contributed individually to such an effort.*

Douglas: *And men and women alike, you had a lot of young men in that, I would assume?*

Harris: *Yes, yes.*

Finding a Church Home

"For me church is real when it gets down to the nitty gritty nub of life where Jesus was in the lives of people."

St. Barnabas soon found itself in a new relationship with St. Luke's. In conversation, the two rectors agreed St. Barnabas had the people, lively worship, and programs. St. Luke's had substantial financial resources and an aging, dwindling congregation. The rector of St. Luke's did not—in his own words—want to become the curator of a museum. They decided to explore the possibility of a merger with their respective vestries. The responses of both were positive. The matter was brought before the two congregations with a largely positive response. With the blessing of the bishop and diocesan standing committee, the merger took place in 1968.

When St. Barnabas was merged with St. Luke's Church, Germantown, in 1968, we lost something of our identity. We all went over to St. Luke's which was a very Anglo-Catholic parish where people worried if you took two steps to the left instead of one and shuddered at the sound of our mixed-voice choir, which I thought was pretty good. They historically had a men and boys choir. Because of living heirs to the donors of its hefty endowments, we were told that we could not append the name of St. Barnabas and had to settle for naming the parish house "St. Barnabas Hall." Subsequently, a St. Barnabas Day School was established and I was pleased by that development.

St. Luke's was too precious and too perfect for me. For me, church just wasn't *real* any more. I felt more like an observer than a participant. Again, for me church is real when it gets down to the nitty gritty nub of life where Jesus was in the lives of people.

So, one morning in July of 1968 I got up and decided I would find somewhere to go to church. I remember thinking that if I didn't go that day, I would never go back, and I couldn't imagine my life without church.

I got in my car with no idea where I was going. I drove to the Church of the Advocate in North Philadelphia. I'd never been there before. It's a huge place, and I didn't realize they were on a summer schedule so I arrived a little before eleven and they were well into a ten o'clock service. Having never been there before, I walked into what I thought was the front door—which turned out to be a side door—and I found myself walking toward an altar in the nave in front of everyone in the congregation. A woman stepped out of her pew, put her arms around me, and I was wrapped in love in that place from that day on. Her name was Jean Harris. I stayed there for twenty years—feeling like it was home.

The choir was great. The people were warm and friendly. The worship was basic and simple and everything about the place, despite its imposing architecture, seemed comfortable and people-centered—due in large part to the rector, Paul Washington, and his wife.

I became very active in that parish and served as a lay reader, vestry member, and finally rector's warden. When the rector went on vacation in August I would read Morning Prayer and preach. Of course clergy would come in to celebrate the Eucharist but many times we just had Morning Prayer and I would prepare and deliver the sermon with no supervision. It was a laid-back kind of place where "all sorts and conditions" of folks came. The sign in the churchyard said, "This church lives the gospel" and it was true. The parish was made up mostly of black people with a sprinkling of whites: it had been at one time all white. However, the neighborhood around the Advocate and indeed, much of the community and the church itself became subject to white flight, and soon the congregation reflected this change.

The Advocate is a huge gothic structure modeled on the Cathedral of Chartres in France. It was built as a memorial to George W. South, the source of whose wealth eludes me, by his widow and daughter after a trip to France. The Souths were Presbyterians and upon completion, the magnificent edifice was offered to the Presbytery of Philadelphia, which decided that it was too ornate for its taste or use. The family lawyer promptly rushed the widow South and her daughter downtown to the diocesan headquarters where they were confirmed on the spot by the bishop and the property was given to the Episcopal Church. The deed of trust specifically states that there can never be anything on that site but an Episcopal Church.

Paul Washington, the rector, became not only my mentor but my dear friend from whom I learned much—three things primarily: what it means to be a loving Christian, to accept people where they were and never to temporize with injustice, nor to make peace with oppression.

In an afterword to Paul's autobiography, *Other Sheep I Have*, I wrote:

> I feel both humble and proud to have been a participant and an observer in so many of the situations that Paul describes with modest understatement and a thorough commitment to honesty. I feel humble, naturally, about those portions of the story that involve me personally. Proud, because the rigorous example set by Paul must have had some impact on my own spiritual formation. This is not to say that other influences and individuals have not been significant in my own spiritual journey, but without question it was in the crucible of service to our Master at the Church of the Advocate during the rectorship of Paul Washington that my own sense of mission and ministry were tested and refined.

Hard Lessons of Privilege

"The damnable thing about institutionalized racism is that well-meaning white folk don't have to do anything overt to insure its perpetuation."

I also learned some valuable lessons early on from my mother. Mom insisted that I attend the Philadelphia High School for

Girls, an all-academic public school, from which I graduated in 1948, having spent four years there. They were not entirely happy years; the work was hard and the administration and teachers unsympathetic to the black girls who were there. Many times I wished I could leave and go to some school where I was wanted and respected, but Mom insisted that since Girls' High was the best school of its kind I had to continue. She put her foot down; I knew there was no use trying to get out of it. "You died to get there and there you will stay. If you can make it there, you can make it for the rest of your life." How true those words would become.

It seemed to be then, and still seems to me now, that the point of school in those days was not really academic at all, but simply an education in snobbishness. The school existed to maintain separations and distinctions among people. Some educators speak of the "hidden curriculum," which schools and universities teach besides the academic subjects. At Philadelphia High School for Girls the curriculum of discrimination was taught rigorously and consistently.

Intellectual snobbishness and superiority were encouraged in subtle manner. Even one of the "pep" songs we sang jokingly reflected this:

Girls High girls are high minded
Bless my soul, they're double jointed.
They work hard and don't mind it
All day long.

Living in that atmosphere toughened us black girls for the challenges that lay ahead, but in the meantime there were many disappointments. For example, we were not allowed to play varsity sports such as field hockey because our teams played suburban schools and it was thought that they would object to encountering black players as equals. So far as I know, the administration didn't ask if our presence was objectionable, they simply assumed it would be. We couldn't be on the swimming team because the swim team practiced at the mid-town YWCA, and black people were not allowed to swim there. When a black girl was elected secretary of the student council, it was announced that the election would be held again. She was not elected that second time. When a black girl made it to the National Honor Society, the chapter of the National Honor Society was abolished with the explanation that it fostered snobbishness. I once received back from a teacher a book report I'd written. She'd given my work a failing grade and wrote very insulting remarks all over it. When I showed the book report to another English teacher she told me that she would have given it an "A."

So there were sympathetic teachers. The racism came from the top and taught us how important it is for decent people to persevere and achieve power, not just so they can change rules, but also so they can change the climate in institutions—not only are the people's attitudes important, but also important is the institutional atmosphere in which those attitudes are expressed.

But things have changed. When a new principal took over at that school, a black girl, one of the close friends to whom this book is dedicated, was soon elected president of the student council, and at our last reunion—my friends and I never miss a reunion—I was asked to give the invocation as a non-distinguished member of the class. In 2006 I was inducted into the court of honor as a distinguished daughter of GHS. And, the principal of the school is now a black woman. Things have come full circle. Hallelujah anyhow!

My mother was right, our perseverance was rewarded, but more importantly those of us who put up with violations of our dignity came together and became the closest of friends. I still see my friends from that time regularly; we travel together and talk on the phone almost every week. We learned to stick together and support each other, so I suppose something good did come of the disappointments and rejection. I'm wary of saying, "It came out all right," because that school treated us very poorly and it hurt. Just because we persevere through racism and grow stronger in the face of discrimination doesn't mean it was right in any way. And I also think it's important for young people today to understand what we endured and how pervasive and open racism was not that many years ago. Today racism is more subtle and institutionalized and therefore more difficult to deal with. It has become part of the fabric of our society—in fact so much so that many do not even recognize it.

The damnable thing about institutionalized racism is that well-meaning white folk don't have to do anything overt to insure its perpetuation. If they just get up every morning and put one foot in front of the other, they will continue to benefit from their unearned white privilege at the expense and denial of people of color. This is especially true for white males. It is also true for white feminists who identify white males as the stumbling block to their advancement and then go home and sleep with the enemy.

On the other hand, to eradicate institutional white racism (and I use "white" deliberately so that everyone understands that people of color lack the power to oppress anybody other than themselves) demands that people take intentional steps to identify how it permeates our society and our global relationships, recognize their own complicity in it and what they can do to dismantle it. It is a continuous and arduous task because few people, if any, want to give up power and few, if any, have heart for the struggle. Fortunately, however, in both church and society, a small but valiant cadre of folk have committed themselves to the task and are taking those first tentative and painful steps that will remove this far-spread cancer from our societal body.

I remember the Rev. Van Bird's words from one of his many powerful sermons and I have appropriated them on several occasions. There is a remnant of God that lives and looks and speaks to the future in the minds of those who understand struggle; in the hearts of those who have dedicated their lives; in the hopes of the people for whom it is waged; in the fears of those against whom it is directed; and in the strength of those who will carry it out.

GHS wasn't all bad. I had a lot of fun with my friends, and I was lucky too. One time I was caught smoking on the roof garden of the school by one of our teachers. I would have been in big trouble if the girl smoking with me hadn't been the president of the senior class. The teacher burst into tears. But in the end she just told us she was so very disappointed and walked away. I figure she couldn't turn me in without turning in the white girl too, so she decided to do nothing. On that day, I got the leftovers of white privilege.

Around this time I was offered a job part-time by the Philadelphia edition of the Pittsburgh Courier, a weekly black newspaper, writing a column, "High School Notes by Bobbie," for which I was paid the grand sum of three dollars a week. I had a great time circulating around the city, press pass in hand, covering local school and teen social events and some other things to which I should probably not have been admitted. This job helped me begin to hone my writing skills, something which came in handy later on in public relations which became the center of the next part of my life.

CHAPTER THREE

The Outsider Within

Throughout most, if not all, of Barbara's professional and vocational journey, she has occupied a standpoint reflective of black women's experience—that of the "outsider within." To be an outsider within suggests that even as one is within a particular institution of power, one's race and gender relegates the individual to a virtual outsider status, regardless of the position they may hold within the institution. Disadvantages notwithstanding, the advantages also loom large. For this standpoint, as identified by sociologist Patricia Hill Collins, is one in which black women in particular are able to "develop a distinct view of the contradictions between the dominant groups actions and ideologies."[1] It is, for example, the domestic worker in the white household being able to see that "the big house" is not what it is cracked up to be. The outsider within, therefore, is able to get to know and learn profound lessons about the power that would keep her marginalized, helping her and others to navigate and thrive within these otherwise oppressive institutions. Most importantly, the outsider within gains the wisdom to dismantle them. This chapter is Barbara's story of being an "outsider within," revealing both the power and the vulnerabilities of being black and female in white patriarchal institutions—including the church.

---

1. Patricia Hill Collins, *Black Feminist Thought: Knowledge, Consciousness and the Politics of Empowerment* (2000; New York: Routledge Classics by Routledge, 2009), 14.

Thriving Against the Odds

"I'll pay you twenty-five dollars a week, even though you aren't worth anything."

After graduation from high school I got a job as a nurses' aid in a nearby hospital. It was tedious and demeaning work, but I needed to be employed. It lasted only a few months because a close friend was being married and the pre-nuptial and post-wedding parties went on for almost thirty days so I decided to chuck it. At age eighteen it didn't seem important. When the partying was over I got serious again and moved on to be the receptionist in the x-ray department of another hospital. This also was a short-lived assignment which I passed on to my sister who kept the position for twenty-six years. The reason my tenure at the hospital was so short was I ,very unexpectedly, was offered a job in a public relations firm by the president of the company. The offer didn't come completely out of the blue, however. Joseph V. Baker, the dean of black public relations consultants, lived in my neighborhood and as a teenager I'd dated his stepson. He said to me, "Quit that job at the hospital, come to work for me, and I'll teach you public relations. I'll pay you twenty-five dollars a week, even though you aren't worth anything."

I arrived at the offices of Joseph V. Baker Associates in a tailored navy blue suit with a starched white blouse and my hair drawn back in a chignon (My hair style changed at different stages of my life as part of my maturing. Finally, hair styling became less and less important and I decided to wear my hair in its natural state. This raised some eyebrows in the corporate world and was looked upon by some as a militant gesture. Not so: it was comfortable, less time consuming and certainly less expensive, and still is). Joe looked at me and said to the staff, "We'll knock the starch out of her inside of two weeks." That evening his wife, having stopped by the office, drove me home. On the way home she told me, "My husband will work the hell out of you." I stayed for nineteen and a half years and spent the last ten years there as president of the company. I left because of philosophical differences with Joe, who was then chairman of the board. I have to say that while at the end he had worked the hell out of me, I had thoroughly learned the trade and I was still pretty starchy—probably more so.

The firm was retained by some of the most distinguished blue chip corporations and trade associations in the country including the Radio Corporation of America (RCA), the Association of American Railroads, Schenley Industries, US Steel Corporation, Hamilton Watch Company, Proctor and Gamble, DuPont, and several others. We counseled them at the point of their approach to the national black community. Early on in that career I attended the Charles Morris Price School of Advertising and Journalism which helped me gain an overview of the PR field and gave me practice in writing concise, clear prose. I never dreamed that in 1973 I would receive an award given to alumni of the school "who have distinguished themselves in their respective fields of endeavor."

Working in public relations was fast paced, interesting, and exciting, but it also meant living out of a suitcase as I crisscrossed the country getting as much as I could out of one railroad ticket. It was nothing to leave Philadelphia and hit Greensboro, Raleigh, Durham, Atlanta, Montgomery, Alabama, New Orleans, and Nashville all on one trip. Similarly, I would head out on assignment for Pittsburgh, Cleveland, Indianapolis, Chicago, Detroit, St. Louis, Kansas City, Oklahoma City, Houston, and Dallas. A West Coast assignment always included a stop in Chicago on the way to Los Angeles with a return out of San Francisco. Sometimes the seasons would change while I was on the road and my mother would ship me the right weight clothing and I would send what I had been wearing back home.

"Interesting" and "exciting" are not quite the words to describe that life in a pressure cooker. Actually, it was crazy, and I often wondered, "what's a nice girl like me doing in a place like this?" That thought certainly crossed my mind as I sat alone

for three hours in the "colored" waiting room of a train station in the middle of the woods, in the middle of the night in
Chehaw, Alabama with two suitcases and a portable typewriter
as my only protective gear. I had been visiting Tuskegee Institute (now University) some ten miles away and the taxi that
had dropped me off was long gone. I kept running through the
worst-case scenarios as I anticipated the momentary arrival of
some night riders in white hoods. Such concern was not completely unfounded since the Ku Klux Klan had staged a cross
burning at the gates of the school not long before.

Tuskegee, founded by educator Booker T. Washington,
remains one of the foremost historically black colleges and was
renowned for its superb choir under the direction of conduc-
tor and arranger William Dawson. It also was the home of the
Tuskegee airmen, the all-black World War II fighter pilot unit
that distinguished itself in combat over Italy. A more unsavory
chapter in its history came about through the thirties and early
forties with the government-sponsored experiments that left
scores of black men untreated to determine the effects of vene-
real disease on that segment of the population. The school was
one of numerous predominately-black college campuses I visited on behalf of client corporations that sponsored scholarship
competitions, awards programs, and convocations and sought
to recruit engineers and other professional employees.

Hectic though those years were, I made some good friends
all over the country, met scores of interesting and prominent
people, and had many rich experiences, some of which were
more than a little hair-raising. Like the time I was on a blind
date with a college professor and his car got pulled over by the
Atlanta police. This was hazardous, to say the least, in Fulton
County, Georgia in the fifties. I'm not so sure I would like to
test it today either. Or when I arrived at the home of the state
NAACP president in Little Rock, Arkansas the day after the Klan
had burned a cross on her front lawn and she and her husband
were being protected by armed guards. The woman was Daisy

Bates, who may be remembered as the person who escorted nine young black boys and girls as they walked past National Guard troops and screaming white parents and became the first students to integrate Central High School in Little Rock.

The city of Dallas seemed to provide my all-time lows. There the lock was picked on my hotel room door; I awoke to find a half clothed man silently snaking his way toward my bed. I opened my mouth, but nothing seemed to come out. After what seemed an eternity I managed to ask, "What do you want?" "Nothing," he replied and hurriedly left. I related the incident to the rector of my parish who asked, "Do you think he came to rob you?" My reply was simply "if he did, he didn't have any pockets in which to put my money." On a subsequent visit to Dallas, I was raped in a motel that was one of few accommodations available to blacks whose travels took them to that city. Blacks were not allowed to shop at Neiman Marcus. The Dallas-Fort Worth airport reluctantly admitted me to its dining room only because I was in the company of a white man, an executive of one of our client companies.

One of my saddest experiences in that city occurred in the old Aldophus Hotel while I was traveling with a client. I went there to meet with him and one of his local corporate representatives. Arriving at the height of the cocktail hour I inquired for my travel companion's room—which was the only place we could really meet over a meal. The astonished desk clerk whimpered, "You mean you're going right up?" The black female elevator operator nearly fell out of her cab as she tried to see where I was going and the older black room service waiter who came to the suite to take our order for cocktails and food looked at me as if I had disgraced the entire race. They all assumed I was there for illicit purposes. It was unthinkable that my presence could be for some legitimate business. That whole experience vividly came to my mind a few years ago as I exited a Cambridge hotel about three thirty in the morning en route to the monastery chapel of the Society of St. John the Evangelist for their Great Vigil of

Easter which gets underway around four in the morning. A maintenance worker polishing up the elevator doors gave me a knowing glance and a smirk that intimated he knew what I had been up to. In both instances, a black woman in a hotel at an unexpected time or place had to be doing something lewd and illicit.

Douglas: *I want to go to one more, sort of, sore subject in your life, perhaps painful but again a blip, but it says something about who you are, even as you just briefly skim over it, and that is this rape. How did that shape you?*

Harris: *Mostly, I was embarrassed that I put myself in a situation where I had let my guard down. And because it occurred where it did, I never reported it.*

Douglas: *Oh, see I was going to ask you whatever happened.*

Harris: *No, it occurred in Dallas, Texas. And because it was there, I never reported it and I never, it was not until recent years that I even shared it with my best friends.*

Douglas: *So no one knew, you held that?*

Harris: *I held it for years. I held it for years.*

Douglas: *Didn't tell your family?*

Harris: *No, I told no one. As I said, it happened during a business trip and the man had escorted me back to my motel and I was talking to him, ending the conversation, and just absentmindedly inserted the key in the lock of my motel room door and I turned to shake his hand and say good night, and he unlocked the door, pushed me in, and he slammed the door shut. And then I realized what was going on and I tried to get back to the door, he chased me around the room, and the next think I knew, he was a big man, slammed me on the bed and raped me and then quickly left.*

Douglas: *But you knew this man?*

Harris: *Well, I didn't know him well. I had had an interview with him.*

Douglas: *You knew enough to be able to have reported him and knew who he was?*

Harris: *Yeah, yeah.*

Douglas: *And even told his place of employment?*

Harris: *Oh absolutely! But, um, I was, one, I was too embarrassed and too fearful.*

Douglas: *Fearful that they would, cause this guy was white?*

Harris: *No this guy was black.*

Douglas: *Oh really?*

Harris: *But to report that to the Dallas police in the 1950s was not a risk I was willing to take.*

Douglas: *Cause what did you think would happen?*

Harris: *I was afraid that they would do something to me. (Long Pause). And I never saw that man again in life or had any reason to be in any contact when I was again in Dallas, Texas but I'll never forget it.*

Douglas: *So how did you, how did that shape you? Again this says something about you, again the strength of who you are. It says something about your resolve because how did, most women don't move on from that, how did that, how did you hold that inside, and how did you not let that pervert your sense of not only self but, jaundice you in your relationships particularly with men, and in your relationships with others. How did you hold that?*

Harris: *Well, for a while I really kind of chastised myself about how I could have been so off-guard and so foolishly off-guard and trusting of a business acquaintance, that a business encounter would be transgressed. I was angry not only with the man, but I was angry with myself, which is why, perhaps, I suppressed it as long as I did.*

Douglas: *And now as you look back, what perspective do you have on that? And what made you, what compelled you finally to tell somebody?*

Harris: (*Long Pause*). *I shared it with my two best friends in a conversation that I guess had to do with Dallas, Texas. And I don't recall now how that came about. But why I mentioned it after decades, I don't know, when we had over the years shared so much of our lives, my God, we've been friends for seventy-one years, and have shared so much of our lives, but I suppose maybe after all these years I was still trying to suppress my own carelessness.*

Douglas: *Have you forgiven yourself?*

Harris: *I think I have now, but I guess I didn't for a long time.*

Douglas: *Did you forgive him?*

Harris: *No.*

Douglas: *You've not forgiven him?*

Harris: *Never forgiven him, no.*

Douglas: *I want to come back to this idea of forgiveness but let me ask you this, if this was something you had not talked about for years, why did you put it in, we wouldn't even be having this conversation if you didn't put in the manuscript?*

Harris: *Well I, I put it in, I'm not sure why I put it in, except that it came to me as part of my stories of travel all over this country and that was one of the incidents that took place in Dallas, Texas where I had another little unsavory incident, but nothing physically overt.*

Douglas: *Tell me this, was there anything that when you walked away that you were able to affirm yourself and stay positive?*

Harris: *What I affirmed was, that I would never take advantage of a person, I would never take advantage of a person, not just physically but because I had some control in a situation that they didn't.*

Douglas: *Did that incident ever in anyway cause you to question God or your faith?*

Harris: *I guess my question out of that whole thing was (Long Pause) . . . Why did I think that man would have respect for me as a business associate and not take advantage of my obvious physical weakness? How could he disrespect me so?*

Douglas: *And did that have anything to do with any development of your own ministry especially in relationship to women?*

Harris: *I can't make a direct connection to ministry but, it certainly heightened my consciousness about how women can be taken advantage of, not realizing that they have put themselves into a vulnerable position.*

Making It in A Man's World

"You've got balls!"

In the course of my travels I did discover something interesting about the South: in those days a black woman who acted a little crazy could sometimes get away with behavior not usually tolerated. For example, I was on a train headed to New Orleans and we were passing through Mississippi about the time I went into the dining car. A bare table behind a green curtain was set aside for "colored" people. The dining car steward said, "Right this way; I have a table reserved for you." "Oh," I said, "in whose name is the reservation?" He, of course, said it was for me, no matter my name. "But," I protested, "this is a table for four and I am only one. I'll take one of these nice little tables for two." After some continued exchange on that level he blustered, "Look lady, I'm from the North and it doesn't make any difference to me, but down here it's the law." "Well," I countered, "if it doesn't make any difference to you, it doesn't make any difference to me. I'll just sit here at this table for two." So I ate breakfast in the middle of the dining car in Hattiesburg, Mississippi, as people sat with their mouths open while their eggs got cold.

The West Coast was where they really lived it up in the corporate world. What was done in other places seemed to be done to excess there. Folks worked hard in the morning because what was not done by noon probably was not going to get done that day. The three-martini lunch was a reality for nearly everybody, except that three martinis served in small decanters turned into six. The executives then hit the golf course in the afternoon while secretaries and other support personnel nodded at their desks. On one trip to Los Angeles I encountered an editor from a popular national magazine in the train's club car. He offered to buy me a drink and, trying to appear the circumspect young business woman rather than some cheap pick up (which seemed to be the first assumption one had of a black woman) I politely declined. Well, a few days later while at lunch at the then-famous Brown Derby restaurant, the editor appeared with actor Orson Welles in tow. Like a fool I started wildly waving my hand in recognition, hoping for an introduction to a movie idol. That guy looked right past me without even a hint of recognition as he made his way to a preferred table for what I am sure was his three-martini lunch. The moral of this story: remaining circumspect can be grossly overrated.

There was another interesting thing I noticed about corporate life. Even high-ranking white men cowered in the face of power. I was in a meeting with the president and chairman of the board of one of our New York City-based client companies. The president, to whom I had seen lesser lights defer, never opened his mouth during that whole session with the chairman except to say hello and to introduce me. It was an eye-opening hoot.

On another occasion, at that same corporation, the chairman was about to leave his office for the day. An elevator was summoned so that he did not have to wait and the word was whispered down the corridor, "He's coming, he's coming." I watched six-foot-tall adult males flatten themselves against wallpaper like prepubescent boys in the presence of Miss Universe.

The journalism training and my years with JVB Associates all stood me in good stead when in 1968, the director of public relations for Sun Oil Company called to say "we're not sure what you can do for us or what we would call you, but I think we need you." He then asked me to put on paper what I would do, what I should be called, and suggest how much salary I needed to do it. My momma didn't raise any fools so I put something together and they bought the whole package. Thus, I became community relations consultant for Sun Oil, at that time the fourth- or fifth-largest petroleum company in the nation. I actually went through a series of titles and assignments for Sun as it went through a merger and several subsequent re-organizations. In 1973, I became manager of Public Relations for the Products Company, which was about 75 percent of the business, the remainder being exploration and production. My department handled relationships with the press, consumers, dealers and distributers, government, and the general public, as well as internal communications for the refining and marketing end of the business.

I will never forget the Friday afternoon I was called to nineteen (the top floor) to find the senior executives gathered in the office of the president of the products division. He said, "We think it's time for a public relations person to head the Public Relations department." Most of the PR managers had come from what we called "the line." They were engineers and other management types mostly. I said, "I don't know the oil business that well." And the response was, "We can teach you the oil business. We need someone who knows PR. You don't have to answer right away. You can let us know Monday morning." So that's how I became manager of Public Relations.

You can imagine the stir my appointment created within and outside the company. One former department member who had moved on to the new corporate headquarters and who only half-jokingly called me "Sister X," remarked, "Well, now, sister has got the whole thing." Of course folks in the black community were quite proud as they read about it in *Jet* magazine and other media—black and white—and realized that one of their own had made it into the ranks of corporate management. And around the country I got "Right on," which was the seventies equivalent of a high five.

Prior to the appointment, a couple of other interesting things happened. I became the first woman president of the Philadelphia chapter of the Public Relations Society of America, of which I was an accredited member, and later vice president of its Foundation for Public Relations Research and Education. I also was elected to membership in the prestigious Public Relations Seminar, a self-perpetuating group of top corporate, trade organization, and agency PR executives. The Seminar, which met annually in posh resort facilities around the country, usually elected only one person from a given corporation or organization to membership. Sun's PR director, who had initially hired me was already "in," so my election was somewhat unusual.

The value of the Seminar was in the opportunity to exchange trade information with high-level operatives in the field and in the quality and caliber of distinguished speakers who addressed the group. I do remember, however, that on one occasion a prominent New York senator showed up with a colossal hangover. Looking like an unmade bed, he completely misread his audience (he thought we were a bunch of salespeople in convention) and was met with stony patrician silence.

As we moved from Pebble Beach, California, to Ponte Vedra Beach in Florida and from The Wigwam in Phoenix to the Greenbrier in West Virginia, again mine was typically the only face of color—other than those of the housekeeping and maintenance staffs. This brings me to an observation: black people learn to live in two cultures. Certainly I lived in the predominately, overwhelmingly white business world and also with my family, friends and church. Many black people had to do so. Churches and organizations were places to which we could repair, have our own identity, and where we could be somebody. This was absolutely necessary if you were going to keep your sanity, integrity, and maintain self-respect. Certainly it was true for me.

For example, when I went off to the Executive Management Program at Penn State University, the first woman from Sun to do so, I lived in a fraternity house with twenty-four white men for the whole time. When I finished I met some friends for a weekend getaway and I just grabbed one and said, "Man, am I glad to see you. I haven't had anybody to talk shit with in weeks," That's what you do when you're in your own cultural milieu. You can say and do things you wouldn't do with people of another culture and still be understood.

Young African Americans today are more prone to express who they are wherever they are. Things have changed that much. For my generation that was not the case. I remember the first time I wore a dashiki and an African turban to Sun Oil Company. Some of the blacks who worked there gasped when they saw me. They weren't sure how people were going to react to it. At the same time I let my hair go natural—no hot irons or relaxers to make it look more like white folk's hair. The same guy who called me Sister X kept asking, "What do black people want?" I answered, "The same things you want." I started giving him books to read, like Eldridge Cleaver's *Soul on Ice* and *The Autobiography of Malcolm X*. Eventually he stopped asking, I think he perhaps got some answers he didn't want.

I was associated with Sun Oil for twelve-and-a-half years and was able to do a few things of which I was pardonably proud. I got the company to transfer the life insurance it carried on employees to a major black-owned insurance company, a bit of a coup if I do say so myself. The deal was marked by my taking a group of Sun management folk to Durham, North Carolina to meet, lunch with, and to tour the operation of the insurance firm. It was the first time any of them had seen a first-rate black corporation and they were stunned. The insurance executives, whom I knew well from my days with the PR firm, put on quite a show and they treated me like a queen.

Secondly, I managed to get the Rev. Jesse Jackson in for a meeting with Sun's senior executives in the boardroom. He was visiting Philadelphia. I found a hole in his schedule and prevailed upon him through his manager to come. Brother Jesse, who credited me with being "the spook who sat by the door," gave them an earful and afterwards one executive said to me, "I'm glad the reverend didn't pass the collection plate because he would have cleaned out my wallet." In addition I helped to establish a minority enterprise small business investment company (MESBIC) as a Sun subsidiary and served on its board of directors. The company made loans to minority owned businesses which enabled many to expand staff, facilities and inventories, thereby making them more competitive.

With the help of four white women and three other black women, all of whom held responsible positions, a Sun Women's Organization was started to help female employees advance in the corporate ranks. We met regularly with senior management and fed them information we thought they needed to accomplish this. As an initial gesture we each bought and presented an executive with a copy of Rosabeth Moss Kanter's book, *Men and Women of the Corporation*.

Lastly, I staged a Youth Enrichment Symposium that brought together two young people from every state in the union and at least one from each foreign country in which Sun conducted business. The latter included Canada, Germany, Japan, England and Venezuela. Sun refinery managers and regional and district marketing people were asked to choose two high school students from their area with the only stipulation that one be female and one a minority. The selection process was left to their discretion.

The young people gathered in Philadelphia for several days for workshops, addresses, and some education and recreational trips to New York City and the nation's capital. The symposium, dubbed YES, was a huge success without much support from management. When I asked what the budget limit for the program was, I was told, "There is no budget." So after I had spent one hundred thirty-two thousand dollars, I just stopped counting and kept on spending.

Although I had a successful career, ending as a senior staff consultant at corporate headquarters when I left following ordination to the diaconate in 1979, I could never quite conform to the corporate discipline. It was something like the military in that, at least back then, you worked through a chain of command. You had to get permission from the captain to talk to the sergeant. I was never comfortable with that. Sun also was a pretty straight-laced, some might even say uptight, organization. The (Presbyterian) influence of the founding Pew family was very much felt, particularly from its then-patriarch J. Howard, and not much levity was tolerated. The irrepressible humor of many on the PR staff, including myself, was regarded as not fitting the corporate mold.

In addition, you were not to exceed your position or status. Sometime after my move to corporate headquarters I bought a smart looking pale green BMW; I had no problem parking it in among the rows of Mercedes the company provided for its ranking executives. The vice president to whom I reported, however, remarked to me, "Don't think it hasn't been noticed that you drive a more expensive car than some of your betters." I looked at him and said, "Who the hell around here is my better?" I then remembered that he drove a Buick. Come to think of it, I recall my mother often telling me I needed to learn to keep a civil tongue in my head.

In a major corporation you really had to have a godfather who served as mentor and looked out for your interests as well. Luckily I had a good one. But frankly, as I look back I don't remember being bowled over by any intellectual giants when I worked there.

When I got to corporate headquarters I realized that I was more comfortable as a consultant because I really chaffed at the corporate discipline. I did what I had to do, but I never really enjoyed it as I had enjoyed the public relations agency. My life there was less structured and when I met with a client I was the most knowledgeable person in the room on the subject about which I was talking. I had real confidence there and knew that I wouldn't get lost in a reorganization, which was a way of life in the corporation.

Once, for example, I got a call asking me if I would take a ten-month leave of absence to come to the Virgin Islands to run the PR piece of a gubernatorial campaign. It was a tempting offer, especially since it came on a cold day in January, but I refused because I knew that when I came back to the company I might not have a seat. Reorganizations were fast and furious and you had to stay on your toes. One man was sent on a temporary assignment to Puerto Rico; when he returned he didn't have a job. Frankly I think the temporary assignment was bogus to begin with and it was an easy way to unload him.

Actually, I've never really had to look for a job. They have just sort of come to me. Of course, there was a glass ceiling that to some degree still exists for blacks and women and certainly I knew I would never make it to the boardroom. And it could be lonely, especially for me. At one executive conference I was the only woman and the only person of color present out of eighty people. We met in a hotel and broke at points into small groups. Each group had to send a spokesperson to talk to the panel of top executives. That meeting was sent via video back to the small groups. In what appeared to be a magnanimous gesture, I was selected to be the spokesperson for my group. And certainly that way none of my colleagues had anything to lose. When I returned to the room where the group was, one of the men said, "You've got balls" (which was a pretty funny thing to say to a woman). He had noticed that when one of the executives had asked me a stupid question I'd looked at him over the rim of my eyeglasses as if to say "you dumb S-O-B." I told him he was right, that's exactly what I was thinking.

In the meantime, I tried to give some time and attention to the community. I served for several years as a trustee of the Seybert Institution, a charitable foundation established by Charles and Maria Seybert for the support of poor boys and girls, and as a member of the board of the Advocate Community Development Corporation, a church-based initiative to build affordable housing for low-income families which was founded by Christine Washington, my rector's wife. As Paul told it, a family had been evicted from their home and the circumstances disturbed Christine greatly. One night she woke him and said, "Paul, we have to build some houses for our people." He replied, "Yes, baby," and went back to sleep The next morning Christine started on her mission and the community development corporation known as ACDC was born. From a modest beginning that few thought would succeed, Christine drove the enterprise to a corporation worth several millions of dollars. Beginning with a handful of modest houses on Page Street, a few blocks from the church, ACDC developed blocks of new houses, rehabilitated scores of deteriorated multi-family dwellings, built an apartment for senior citizens on the site of a former public school, and rebuilt a condemned apartment building for homeless and disabled persons. It was an honor to be a part of such an undertaking.

In addition, I served on the Public Committee for the Humanities in Pennsylvania, the board of the Conference of Christians and Jews, and the boards of Penn Center Academy, an alternative high school housed in the YMCA, and the Ile Ife Black Humanitarian Center, a community cultural outreach program for black youth.

Meanwhile, I was also very engaged with the church, which was increasingly becoming caught up in the issues of society. I was busy serving on the diocesan council, Episcopal Community Services, the social work arm of the diocese, and several other committees. While I had been attending the triennial General Conventions of the church for several years to work on various progressive issues, I had never been a regular deputy. In 1979 I was elected a lay deputy from Pennsylvania. Interestingly enough, that year our four-member lay deputation was comprised of three women and one man.

At the national church level I was tapped for the first board for Clergy Deployment (which finally came into being a few years after the South Bend Special General Convention, which I speak about in the next chapter); the board of the Development Committee, which was ironically—for me at least—led by the late Oscar Carr, a wealthy Mississippi cotton planter. I was also on the Commission on Black Ministries; the Commission on Social and Specialized Ministries; the committee to evaluate the General Convention Special Program; and the board of the short-lived Absalom Jones Theological Institute, a component of the Interdenominational Theological Center in Atlanta.

Even though overall I enjoyed my life in business and some of the perks that came with it, there was something missing that the church seemed to speak to for me.

Moreover, as I described earlier, the corporate culture—brimming with the subtle and not-so-subtle realities of racism and sexism—was a bit too backbiting and toxic for me. I'm sure life is much different in that orbit these days. Given some recent corporate debates, however, there are probably an equal number, if not more, of folk we referred to as "smiling cobras or praying mantises." Oh well, Hallelujah, anyhow!

I don't always serve Him as I should.
I don't deserve so much good
So many things are not as they should be
But God is so good to me.

—Doris Akers, "God Is So Good to Me"

CHAPTER FOUR

A Jesus Movement for Freedom

ichael Curry, the twenty-seventh presiding bishop and primate of the Episcopal Church, has called the Episcopal Church to renew its commitment to be a part of the Jesus Movement. This is a movement not to bring people into the church, but one in which the church goes to the people—as Jesus did—and reflects what indeed it means to be a follower of Jesus. To be such a follower does not require one to talk about Jesus. Rather, it requires that one carries forth the ministry of Jesus to "do justice," so to bring the world closer to the "Kingdom of God" about which Jesus preached. The Jesus Movement is about nothing less than being the very movement of Jesus in our times.

There are times in which the Jesus Movement is palpable, even in the midst of brutal and violent injustice. Such were the times during the civil rights movement in the 1960s. Through the stories that she tells, Barbara Harris provides us with on-the-ground realities of the hard-fought struggles and dangerous challenges of what it means to be a part of the Jesus Movement, and thus of the faith that is required. After reading her words, there was nothing more left to say. And so this chapter is precisely how she first wrote it without any added conversation.

Fighting to Be Free

"My God, here come a red-head nigger."

The early to mid-sixties was an interesting time. The civil rights movement was in full swing, the push for change in the air was contagious and there was even the feeling among some of us that we could make a difference in society. Leaders who offered hope were emerging and it indeed seemed a *kairos* moment.

In Philadelphia, a persuasive Baptist minister, the Rev. Leon Sullivan, had mobilized black clergy around the city to lead their congregations in boycotting products manufactured by companies that refused to hire or promote qualified minority employees to responsible positions. That initiative was successful and the employment picture began to change. Sullivan went on to establish a job training program called the Opportunities Industrialization Center (OIC), which helped people develop marketable basic skills in a number of fields. He had a Midas touch and the OIC model became highly successful for what it was. The program, which won financial and other support from American industry, spread to other cities and eventually to some African countries. Sullivan himself won a seat on the General Motors board of directors, becoming one of the first African Americans to join corporate America at that level.

Meanwhile, Martin Luther King Jr. was proclaiming his dream and after the success of the Montgomery bus boycott and the 1963 March on Washington, some thought there was a possibility of it coming true in their lifetime. That was before people gained a clear understanding of the pervasive nature of systemic racism, and the grim reality of institutional resistance to change set in.

The Student Non-Violent Coordinating Committee (SNCC) was heading in a new direction as it moved away from lunch counter sit-ins and began to focus on voter education and registration and other political activity in the deep South. New voices were challenging the old established leadership of organizations such as the NAACP and the National Urban League. And it was primarily the students who heard and recognized the faint sound in the background as the muffled, impatient rumblings of the emerging Black Power movement that was to open a chapter in race relations which this country could scarcely imagine. During that period the year 1965 was particularly important to me and two things remain indelibly stamped on my consciousness—the Selma to Montgomery march and a summer spent working with the Delta Ministry in Greenville, Mississippi.

I participated in only a small part of the fifty-mile march from Selma to Montgomery. Several of us who were part of the Philadelphia chapter of the Episcopal Society for Cultural and Racial Unity (ESCRU) joined with clergy and lay people from predominantly black denominations to fly to Alabama and join the marchers en route. The local leadership of the African Methodist Episcopal church, including its bishop, had chartered a plane which they had no trouble filling. Little did we know what lay in store. Had we known, we may not have been so eager to be a part of that piece of history.

For some senseless reason I had gone from having a few blonde streaks in my hair to a dye job that turned out some hideous shade of bright orange. The minute I got off the plane and started through the airport, one local good ol' boy pointed to me and announced loudly, "My God, here come a red-head nigger." That was the least of it. Heading up Dexter Avenue in Montgomery the last day of the march we heard unbelievable obscenities shouted by women with young children in their arms. Most of it was directed at white participants who were regarded as traitors and called "nigger lovers." Even nuns were accused of sleeping with black men who were part of the march.

One or two other incidents stand out in my mind. As people cursed and made obscene gestures, many of the marchers waved and blew kisses to the bystanders, some of whom turned away in utter disbelief. As the speeches were being made from the steps of the Alabama state capitol building, the day grew warm. Someone started passing a huge mason jar of ice water through the crowd near me. It had been provided by the good women of Dexter Avenue Baptist Church where Dr. King was pastor. The water passed from black hands to white, from Christian lips to

Jewish and someone whispered "We are having Holy Communion right here in the middle of the street."

Following the march, we stood on a vacant lot at a street corner, waiting for buses to take us to the airport for our chartered return home. It was everybody's hope to get out of Montgomery proper before dark. At about five o'clock the regular army troops departed, followed by the Alabama National Guard. Next the state troopers pulled out, the local police went home to supper and there we stood—praying that the buses would get there immediately, if not sooner. At that moment I noticed a light colored car driven by a woman. I remarked to the person nearest me, "Who is that down here with Michigan license plates? She's a sitting duck." I had no way of knowing the woman was Viola Luizzo of Detroit, who shortly afterwards was shot and killed on the highway as she ferried some young black men back to their homes in Lowndes County where the march had begun. We made it to the airport only to find that the plane had not been permitted to taxi to the terminal, nor would it be fueled locally. We walked to the edge of the airfield by flashlight, boarded the plane by some rickety metal stairs, made it to Atlanta to buy jet fuel and took off for home. I learned of the grim highway slaying as we disembarked back in Philadelphia about three in the morning. We were safely home, but the bitterest battles were just beginning.

That same year I spent my summer vacation time working as a volunteer with the Delta Ministry, a program of the National Council of Churches serving the fertile delta region of Mississippi. Among its activities were voter registration and education, a risky undertaking in that state. And it was not just risky for the volunteers, but for the people who had to live there after the volunteers had gone home.

Interestingly, the program's associate director was the Rev. Warren H. Mckenna, who by that time had already served several congregations in the diocese of Massachusetts. The person with whom I planned to work was a black Episcopal priest, the

Rev. Harry J. Bowie, who headed the office in McComb. On the Saturday night before my scheduled Monday morning departure for cotton country, Bowie called to say that the McComb office had been fire bombed and since they had no way to protect me I should report instead to the Greenville office. I rearranged my travel and on the Atlanta to the Greenville leg of the journey met up with the Rev. Albert "Kim" Dreisbach, who at that time was a field secretary for ESCRU. Kim offered encouragement and sound advice as we winged our way toward what was to be one of the most desperate situations I had ever encountered.

This was my first time on Mississippi soil and to me, a big-city-bred Northerner, it was like being in an underdeveloped country. Frankly, I had seen poor people before, but was not prepared for the almost primitive way some black folks were living. One could see through sparsely furnished shacks from front to back and the barest of necessities seemed to be lacking, including indoor plumbing.

Some workers on cotton plantations had gone on strike and had been evicted from the land by angry farmers. They had established a tent city on the outskirts of town and families were living hand-to-mouth in unsanitary conditions. They had, how-ever, jerry-rigged some electricity, tapping into overhead power lines, and some of the tents even boasted a TV set.

The working conditions on the plantations were reminis-cent of sharecropping days where one ended the year owing more to the famer than one ostensibly had earned. Sadly the strikers seemed virtually powerless, because for every one who left a job, there were at least three needy others in line to take their place. Even women drove tractors from sunup to sun-down, leaving small children at home behind locked doors to fend for themselves.

I lived fairly comfortably with a self-employed black beauti-cian, one of the few people who could house civil rights work-ers without danger of losing a job. Again, I was not accustomed to houses without basements and I found it curious, to say the least, that in winter she stored coal in her bathtub. There was a thin film of coal dust that was impossible to remove, and she and her family had learned to live with it, but I must admit it was disconcerting for me.

Many of the volunteers were college students and all were white. I was something of a curiosity and got a lot of strange looks from blacks and whites. By the way, I had gotten rid of the orange hair and was almost back to my normal appearance. I say "almost" because the hair, while back to its natural dark brown, after repeated dyeing resembled matted straw.

Perhaps the best way to describe my Delta Ministry experience and something of what it meant to me is to share part of a Lenten homily titled "I'll Never Forget," delivered more than thirty years later.

In addition to voter registrations, a part of my task was to help lay the groundwork for a boycott of local beverage distributors who were guilty of overt and blatant racist practices against black store owners. As a stranger in the community and an "uppity" northern black woman, this was a somewhat risky way to spend my summer vacation. The year before—known as Freedom Summer—three young civil rights workers had been killed in Philadelphia, Mississippi and their bodies hidden in a dam. Goodwin and Schwerner were from New York and Cheyney was a local person. Prior to that, prominent Mississippi NAACP leaders Medgar Evers and Vernon Dahmer had been killed by members of the Klan. So obscure little old Barbara Harris, along with other volunteers, was an easy target.

Danger was real and imminent and we were instructed to take precautions as we went about our daily round. We were told, for example, the only safe taxies in which to ride, what not to say on the telephone, the route to take from one part of town to another, and the like. I would be less than honest if I did not admit to having second thoughts and moments of failing courage. One day two of us wandered off of a state road onto the road of a cotton plantation and were chased by some shotgun-toting men in a pickup truck.

But what I never will forget, out of all that total experience, is a modern day Judas who lived in the heart of the Greenville community, just as Judas Iscariot was within the close circle of those in the company of Jesus. This Judas walked with a limp, dragging his right foot as he moved. To say that he was physically unattractive would be a gracious and generous statement. Perhaps his appearance was a contributing factor to his behavior and his actions. He was an ugly, loping loner and it was no secret that he was despised by the community. He walked up and down the main street of the black community every day all day long. He walked and he watched. He watched the office, he watched who came and went and he watched who went where. As I walked down one side of the street, he walked down the other. As I made my way back up the street, he followed along on the other side, watching, always watching. He looked in windows where people went and when he was not walking he sat in the local restaurant and watched.

Every night he attended the rallies and meetings held in the black churches. He sang the hymns and freedom songs. He bowed his head for the prayers, he listened to the testimony and he watched who was there. And after we had sung and after we had prayed and after we had testified, he left. He left to go and report to the chief priest, in this case the chief of police, on what he had seen and what he had heard. And for his reporting he received the grand sum of two dollars—not much more than thirty pieces of silver.

Just as Jesus' Judas had his reasons for betrayal, so—I am sure—Greenville's Judas had his. I can only speculate about such life situations as dashed hopes, unfulfilled aspirations, lack of alternatives, reasons and dead ends that drove him. Whatever might have moved him to betray his own oppressed people lay between him and God. But as surely as Judas

Barbara's high school graduation photo

BARBARA HARRIS

July 29, 1974—Barbara serving
as acolyte for the ordination
of the Philadelphia Eleven
*Photo by Brad Hess. Used by
permission.*

February 12, 1989—"moment of consecration"
Episcopal Diocese of Massachusetts *Photo: David Zadig. Used by permission.*

Barbara hugs Paul Washington, mentor and preacher at the event, at her consecration
Episcopal Diocese of Massachusetts *Photo: David Zadig. Used by permission.*

Standing with the Presiding Bishop shortly after her consecration
Episcopal Diocese of Massachusetts *Photo: David Zadig. Used by permission.*

Bishop Harris' formal portrait by Simmie Lee Knox, 2002

Bishops Harris and Tutu, January 2002

Barbara and Nan Peete
at Lambeth
From *The Guardian*

Celebrating Nan Peete's birthday, August 2013 *Photo courtesy of Nan Peete*

Celebrating Nan Peete's birthday, August 2013 *Photo courtesy of Nan Peete*

Bishops Harris and Curry talking together in anticipation of their co-authored book, *In Conversation* *Photo by Ken Davies*

May 13, 2017, speaking at Christ Church—San Marcos in Tarrytown, NY *Photo by Ken Davies*

Iscariot was loved by Jesus, so this man was within the circle of our Lord's embrace as well.

Sadly, I never spoke with him; I never got to know him nor find out anything about his life. Had I been more sensitive, more perceptive, more like the Christ I claim to follow, one day I might have crossed the street and engaged him in conversation. Instead I glared at him like some loathsome leper and I let the opportunity for some Christ-like encounter or some reconciling engagement slip by. Blinded by my own sense of self-righteousness, I was more ready to judge than to understand, more ready to condemn than to forgive; more ready to be right than to be loving. As I look back on that time, I stand chastened and humbled by both the Pennsylvania Dutch truism, "We are too soon old and too late smart," and the biblical admonition, "Judge not lest you be judged."

And while I will never forget the ugly, limping, despicable, and rejected Judas of Greenville, Mississippi, there are other things I must never forget. I must never forget that Jesus of Nazareth died on Calvary for all of humanity—the just and the unjust, the righteous and the unrighteous, the Judases and the Johns, the beloved, even the likes of you and me. I must never forget that no one is outside the circle of God's embrace. I must never forget that by the love of Christ Jesus we all are gathered into the communion of saints. And I will never forget that I must daily strive to be true to our Baptismal Covenant to "seek and serve Christ in all persons . . ." Moreover, I must never forget Jesus' very words to the disciples gathered at that last Passover meal: "A new commandment I give to you, that you love one another; even as I have loved you, that you love one another. By this all will know that you are my disciples if you have love for one another."

From Greenville, I went on to Jackson for the annual national meeting of ESCRU. As we gathered in the old Heidelberg Hotel, we were greeted by the bishop of Mississippi, John M. Allin, who later became the church's presiding bishop. He delivered a message from the local sheriff to the clergy who had visited the city the previous summer on a Freedom Ride, inviting any who were not comfortable in the hotel to come on over to the city jail where the cells they had occupied on their last visit were available. Bishop Allin thought it was amusing. We did not.

Although ESCU was in decline, the meeting did get a boost from an appearance from Fannie Lou Hamer, the plain speaking, no-nonsense black housewife from Ruleville who headed the Mississippi Freedom Democratic Party. She may well be remembered for her response to a newspaper reporter's question asking her to sum up the state of the civil rights movement. She said, "I'm sick and tired of being sick and tired."

The sixties came to a somewhat dismal end in both church and society. Of course 1968 was punctuated by the assassination of Dr. King in Memphis, who in his last book, *Where Do We Go From Here: Chaos or Community*, wondered whether black people were worse off than they had been several years before. His reference was not to open segregation, but to the insidiousness of systemic and institutionalized racism. And indeed many were worse off.

Ironically, I was in Charlotte, North Carolina having dinner at a country club the day Dr. King was killed. The client with whom I was meeting informed me that I was the first black person to dine there. I knew nothing of the assassination until I walked into my home in Philadelphia later that night and the Rev. Jesse Jackson was describing the events of that afternoon on television. A conference with the Philadelphia representative of the same client organization was scheduled for the next day. An early morning telephone call offered me the opportunity to cancel the meeting, my caller saying, "We understand if you don't feel like talking to white people today." The meeting went on as scheduled.

Today it strikes me as strange that I could go through with that meeting, but had difficulty speaking with whites the day following one of the more brutal episodes in the television drama *Roots*. I sat in my office at Sun's corporate headquarters in a quiet rage and waved people away from the door until noon.

In 1969 the Episcopal Church held the second only Special General Convention in its history. This "off year" gathering, held on the campus of Notre Dame University in South Bend, Indiana during the dog days of August, was marked by conflict, confusion and chaos. As one of the "additional representatives," appointed to insure the presence of ethnic minorities, women, and youth to augment the largely white and all-male diocesan deputations, I joined Bishop Robert L. Dewitt, members of the Union of Black Clergy and Laity (UBCL) and others from the diocese of Pennsylvania (UBCL came into being in the summer of 1968).

As we flew to South Bend it became apparent that the diocese of Pennsylvania would play a major part in the drama that would unfold. In our group was Muhammed Kenyatta of the Black Economic Development Conference (BEDC) which had issued its controversial "Black Manifesto" demanding five hundred million dollars from white churches and Jewish synagogues as reparations to African Americans for injustices suffered over the years. The money was to provide capital for such entities as a Southern Land Bank, publishing and printing industries and other cooperative businesses. We chuckled over the fact that the diocese had provided air fare and expenses for Kenyatta who, on the first evening of the convention, would disrupt the proceedings. At a joint session of the House of Bishops and the House of Deputies, the stated agenda of which was to discuss a new system of clergy deployment, Kenyatta wrested the microphone away from then Presiding Bishop Hines and thus began several days of debate on the Manifesto, reparations, and the "black agenda."

Without rehearsing all of the strategy employed to tie up the convention agenda for the next three days, one humorous aspect was that those of us who sat in the "cheap seats"—the additional representatives who took part in the small group meetings, but

not in the discussions on the floor of the convention—kept making meaningless, yet what appeared to be threatening, gestures
which helped to confuse the elected deputies even further and
finally had some leaving their seats and consulting with blacks as
to how they should vote.

One of the points we won at the Special Convention was
the creation of additional seats on the church's national Executive Council to again assure the participation of minorities
and youth. Two seats were awarded to blacks, two to youth
and one each for a Hispanic and a Native American. Blacks
were expected to offer four names for the two seats, so that
members of the Council could pick and choose who our representatives would be. Much to their anger and dismay, we
presented two names only, thus forcing them to accede to an
election already held. In the fall of that year, the Rev. Henson
Jacobs and I joined the Executive Council as representatives
of the UBCL. Some in the church would have preferred the
bogeyman to left-leaning Barbara Harris on that council, not
unlike some in the church today.

The following year we went on to the regular triennial General Convention in Houston where we brokered away the special seats on the council in exchange for some major pieces of
the church's funding pie. We were told that the convention was
aware of the need for minority representation on its governing body and we should "trust the process," that people like
us would be elected. Needless to say, we were not elected and
council looked much like it did before South Bend.

Meanwhile back in the diocese of Pennsylvania retrogres-
sive forces in the church were becoming increasingly unhappy
with Bishop Bob Dewitt because of his liberal positions and
actions, particularly on racial issues. These included his participation in some of the daily marches around the walls of Girard
College, a boarding school for "poor white male orphans"
established in 1848 by the will of wealthy merchant Stephen
Girard. By the mid-sixties the institution, once located on

farmland, was situated in the heart of the now black North Philadelphia community. The demonstrations were aimed at breaking Girard's will so that poor black male orphans might enter the institution as well. In 1968 the United States Supreme Court did rule that the will could be broken and African Americans and other minorities could be admitted to the school, but that is another story.

The increasing dissatisfaction with Bob Dewitt intensified as unidentified groups known as the "Voice of the Catacombs" and "the Renaissance" emerged and became openly critical of diocesan policies and the activities of the bishop and some of his clergy, including my rector Paul Washington. I mention these groups not because they had any real impact or were of importance, but largely because Episcopalians and others, need to know that these cells of disaffected members of the diocese were the precursors of today's so-called traditionalists who selectively honor those portions of church polity that suit their purposes. Oh well, Hallelujah anyhow!

CHAPTER FIVE

An Episcopal First

n her now famous "Ain't I a Woman?" speech delivered in 1851 at the Women's Rights Convention in Akron, Ohio, Sojourner Truth declared, "If the first woman God ever made was strong enough to turn the world upside down all alone, these women together ought to be able to turn it back, and get it right side up again!" On February 11, 1989, before over eight thousand people and sixty-plus bishops, it seemed that one "skinny, nappy-haired black woman," had indeed turned the church on its ear—and perhaps on the course to be set "right side up again!" To be sure, the path to that day signaled that something revolutionary was happening in the church. The question is did Barbara know it? And if she did, when? This chapter tells the story of the journey to that February day.

The Call

"It's taking this man forever to tell me that someone else has been elected."

Douglas: *Barbara, at what point did you realize you were going to be bishop?*

Harris: *I suppose as I was entering, the convention hall as part of the four processions, I was still questioning myself as to how I had gotten to that point and recalling my thoughts all through the process . . . the nominating and electing process . . . that it was interesting to be considered but I never believed it would really go anyplace, until I got the phone call. . . .*

Shortly after the conference on women in the episcopate and while I was serving as executive director of the Episcopal Church Publishing Company, a young woman priest from Allston, Massachusetts, Mary Glasspool (then rector of St. Luke's and St. Margaret's Church and now assistant bishop in the Diocese of New York), called to ask if a group could put my name forward in the nominating process for suffragan bishop in Massachusetts. I prayed hard about it for almost a month and then let her know that I was willing for that to happen. I also asked the Rev. Canon Edward Rodman, who was urban missioner for the diocese of Massachusetts at the time, what he thought of the idea. Ed, in his typically cynical way, said, "Why not? The worst thing that could happen would be that you would get it!"

I didn't think there was a chance in the world that I would be nominated, let alone elected. And that's what I said at each step in the process. Members of the nominating committee came to Philadelphia to hear me preach and I said "well, it won't go any further." They interviewed my references and other people around town and I said to myself, "well, it's flattering to be considered, but it won't go any further." I met with the entire nominating committee, some members whom I knew from other contexts, and I said the same thing. And when the slate of nominees came out with my name on it, I went to Massachusetts to meet with groups of deputies who would be voting in the special diocesan convention at which the election would take place. Such meetings are now graciously called "walkabouts." Back in 1988, they were referred to as "the dog and pony show." During those sessions I thought, "I'll never see these people again in my life, so I can say exactly what's on my mind." And that's just what I did.

And so we went on to the election on Saturday September 25, 1988. I waited at home in Philadelphia—my sister, Joey, and my best friend, Dorothy, with me. Also there that day was a young woman priest from Washington, DC, Gayle Elizabeth

Harris, whom I called "sister-daughter." Gayle had gotten into her car that morning and driven up to be with me. Not only didn't we dream that I would be elected, we never imagined that fourteen years later she would be chosen for the same office and become my successor in the diocese.

I got a phone call after every ballot telling me how things were proceeding. It seemed to be a horse-race between a good priest named Marshall Hunt and myself. Interestingly, Marshall's name was not on the original slate of nominees but came in by petition because some people were not happy that no rectors of cardinal parishes had been proposed.

After the sixth ballot I was told that the next call would probably be from David Johnson, the bishop of Massachusetts. Soon the diocesan receptionist, Helen Robinson, called and said, "Bishop Johnson is on his way from the cathedral and will be with you in a few minutes, so just hold on. He will be calling from the conference room on the first floor." Finally she came back on the line and said, "If you have to go to the bathroom, you can." Then she came on again and said: "He's taking the call in his office, but he is taking the stairs to get there." He was walking up four flights. I said, "It's taking this man forever to tell me that someone else has been elected."

When he finally came on the line he said, "The people have chosen you as suffragan bishop." I was so shocked that it seemed like there was an eternity of silence on my part. I then said, "I humbly accept." Instantly I remembered that you are not supposed to say that right away. You're supposed to say, "I'll pray about it and get back to you." Too late, I had already accepted. I called my mother and said, "Guess what? I've been elected in Massachusetts." Mom's non-committal reply was, "Is this what you want?"

The Road Ain't Easy

"Harriet Tubman remains for me a model of faith, determination and audacity in the best sense of the word."

In November of 1988 I was invited to briefly address the annual diocesan convention held at the cathedral in Boston. My remarks that day still have meaning for me. I said in part:

> I continue to give thanks to God for the courage and the audacity of faith shown by this convention in electing me as your bishop suffragan. I thank you for the confidence expressed in me by that action. The rich outpouring of love, prayer and support in the days leading up to September 24 and since then—from within the diocese, from across the country and, indeed, from far corners of the world has been both heartwarming and humbling and I am deeply moved as it continues.
>
> I am genuinely excited about the prospect and the potential for our life together in this place and what our shared ministry can mean not only for this diocese but for the whole church. And I know that many of you join me in that sense of excitement.
>
> In reflecting on the election over the past few weeks, I have several times been reminded of a familiar passage found in the first chapter of 1Corinthians at verse 27: "But God has chosen what is foolish in the world to confound the wise." Again and again our God, the God of history, has manifested a penchant for doing so in continuing to act in the lives of God's people. How many times have we been confronted with the historical record in this regard, if not actual witnesses to the fact.
>
> Many of you are familiar with the story of Harriet Tubman, the frail and rather sickly young black woman who escaped from slavery, yet returned to the South nineteen times to shepherd over three hundred other slaves to freedom.

Some of her charges were reluctant to shed their shackles because they could not even conceive of the new way of life liberation represented, but she continued in her calling and her quest.

The conventional odds were stacked against this woman who was given to spells of dizziness and seizures. The likelihood of success in her mission was by conventional wisdom, nil. Yet this most unlikely rescuer was used by God and became a Moses to her people.

Harriet Tubman remains for me a model of faith, determination and audacity in the best sense of the word. She is an embodiment of the scripture cited and an example that God can and does use unlikely creatures such as you and me as instruments of reconciliation, vessels of love and channels of his grace.

You have invited me into ministry with you through the office of the bishop. I accept the invitation in the hope that the church will affirm it. Our work together must begin by venturing out on that broad platform of faith. Though we may not see clearly the full pathway that lies before us, we know that God, the God who chooses the foolish things of the world to confound the wise, has brought us safe thus far and we trust our God for the next step of the journey.

Before the actual consecration could happen, however, there was business to be done and difficult business it promised to be. It would be necessary, as part of the procedure, for my election to be publicly certified as consented to by the Episcopal Church. I already knew that sixty-six bishops and jurisdictions had consented to the election and that I had received consents from a majority (a bare majority) of the standing committees of all the dioceses across the country and those in Mexico and the Caribbean which then made up the Ninth Province.

I also knew that there was serious objection from those who were opposed to the ordination of a woman to any clerical position. Some of the opposition was principled and dignified; some was, to say the least, not either of these things. I had lived through controversy before and as a black person, knew the level vilification could reach; still I was frankly surprised at the depth of meanness and obscene rage of some of the objectors.

The consent process was long and difficult. It lasted from the September election to January. One diocese, South Carolina, sent me a set of legalistic questions, even though everyone knew they weren't going to consent anyway. I responded, but also sent them a note suggesting that their questions might be more appropriate if pastoral in nature rather than legal. North Carolina's standing committee voted twice; I got fewer affirmative votes the second time, which I thought was pretty funny. The diocesan newspaper ran my picture with a black slash across my face, like the no-smoking signs, and printed an article which said, "The wrong woman at the right time." A few years ago I was invited to North Carolina to lead a conference on the Baptismal Covenant and I was a co-consecrator of their bishop Michael Curry who was later elected presiding bishop of the Episcopal Church. So things have a way of coming full cycle.

I feel very honestly that people had a right to object and to be strong in their opinions but, once again, it was the viciousness that surprised me. Of course it has been said that "Nobody can hate like Christians." One man wrote, "You stinking black bitch. Stop polluting Massachusetts." His note was accompanied by an ad for a feminine douche. A young priest from South Carolina said in writing that the reason I took the left wing positions on issues I did was because I had not had a liberal arts education. He "reasoned" that if I'd had the benefit of an undergraduate degree, I would be a more reasonable person. My response was that a liberal arts education, coupled with seminary, had not done him much good in view of the fact that he was a signatory of the egregious so-called "Baltimore Declaration" and, I believe, the subsequent "First Promise" statement. These were issued by two predominately male so-called "traditionalist" groups.

Amusingly, a man from Georgia wrote, "I seen you on TV marching around and laughing. You can fool some of the people, but you can't fool Jesus." For months every time my pictures appeared in a magazine, a newspaper or on TV, my sister called to say, "I seen you. . . ."

Along the way I was surprised by the lack of support from people I thought had no axe to grind in my election. There was a black layman in the diocese of New Jersey—whose standing committee voted against me—who volunteered a letter to the national church publication opposing my consecration. He strongly stated the obvious fact that I did not represent him. Of course I didn't represent him, having been elected by Massachusetts, not by New Jersey. The then-bishop gave his consent, but it might be noted that New Jersey is the same diocese which drove out its subsequent bishop with a golden million-dollar handshake. I learned that the Philadelphia chapter of a tony African American women's organization expressed its "regret" that "the first could not have been a better representative of the black community."

Eventually the consents from the dioceses came in, and then the bishops voted and we were able to inform the presiding bishop that majorities had been received. Today the consent process is conducted simultaneously among standing committees and bishops, which certainly is much more expeditious.

After I got to Massachusetts in early January 1989, Bishop Johnson said, "I probably should not ask you this but I'm going to anyway. Are you in a same-sex relationship?" I burst into laughter and answered "No, I am not now, never have been and I don't expect to be." One of my colleagues, who shall remain nameless, suggested I should have said "yes." I asked why and he replied, "David would have jumped out of the fourth floor window and you would have had the diocese all to yourself."

I think Bishop Johnson was scared to death when I was elected, both by the reaction and by me. For some reason he felt terribly threatened by me. I know, for example, that his wife was very upset by my election, feeling that the people of Massachusetts had done a terrible thing to him. I suppose I should have known that he had mixed feelings about me when he decided to walk up those four flights of stairs before talking to me on the phone.

The First Woman Bishop

"Lord, how am I gonna do this?"

Douglas: *When you left that first day, after you went home that first day, what did you think? Did you think, oh Lord what have I gotten myself into?*

Harris: *Basically, I had not yet found an apartment, I was living in a hotel a little bit around the corner from the diocesan offices. And every morning Ed Rodman would meet me and walk me to the office. Every evening he would walk me back to my hotel. For the first little bit.*

Moving to Massachusetts got me away from some of the telephone calls and the death threats, but the hate mail intensified. I had changed my number a few times in Philadelphia but folks did not know where I was living in Massachusetts.

Canon Rodman came to my hotel every morning and walked me to the diocesan office. He also walked me back every evening and gave me this personal protection until I moved into a sublet apartment downtown. Ed, my old and dear friend of over thirty years, was a veteran of SNCC and the civil rights struggle so he knew what was imperative and rose to the moment.

Douglas: *What was your morning like the day you were to be consecrated? In fact, tell me about those last twenty-four hours before you walked to that convention center.*

Harris: *Well I, I don't remember that much of it in detail, except talking with my mother and my sister and the dinner gathering the evening prior. And the excitement that was in the air and I* *remember a few things that were said. I remember Van Bird, my mentor, saying, "God does not choose us because we are finished instruments, but God reshapes and remolds us." And he said that I needed to say to people "be patient with me; God is not through with me yet." And I remember Edmund Browning holding his hands up aloft, and saying, "these hands are ready." My mother and sister and I shared a hotel suite and I think we didn't stay up talking too long that night because I knew it was going to be a long day so I went on to bed at a fairly decent hour, and the morning was so busy, you know, getting to the convention center, and getting vested and all ready for the procession, that there wasn't a lot of time to do a lot of thinking. It was just busy time. You know, wondering to myself how things were shaping up, was the service going to go well, that there were going to be all these processions and were they going to manage and handle all of that, I just wasn't sure how this was all going to come together and be pulled off and I was totally unprepared, when I walked in, for the number of people that were there. That took my breath away.*

Douglas: *What did you expect?*

Harris: *Well I expected, you know, a few thousand just because the diocese was so big but I wasn't prepared for people from all over being there. A bishop from the Church of South India, we had no idea was coming, a bishop from Rupert's Land, we had no idea he was coming. People, lay people, from across the nation.*

Douglas: *Did you understand the magnitude of what was going on? Did that sink into you?*

Harris: *Not until that morning.*

Douglas: *And what did you come to understand?*

Harris: *That I was stepping into a role the historic proportions of which I would never have dreamed of.*

Douglas: *Did you have any fear and trembling when that came to you?*

Harris: *Oh yeah. I wondered, Lord, how am I gonna do this? Because I still was not sure of what it was I was being called to do!*

Douglas: *In what sense of that?*

Harris: *Well, I didn't know all of the proportions of the role of being a bishop. Particularly among people I did not know. (Long Pause). I guess I perhaps was thinking, "how am I gonna do this?" Except I, at the press conference afterwards, I think I was asked how I would handle my detractors and I just said I'm going to do the best that I can to fulfill this office. And that's what I set out to do.*

The consecration took place on the eleventh of February. It was a great day. A great day not just for me, not just for women, not just for African Americans, but, I believe, for the whole church. Not only had a centuries-old barrier been broken, but the genie was out of the bottle and—despite the church's long held belief in a process of reception for controversial breaks with tradition—there was no going back.

As the consecration service opened I was dazzled by the spectacle—the eight thousand five hundred people gathered in the auditorium of the Hynes Convention Center in Boston, the rows of bishops, sixty-two of them, the hundreds of clergy from all over the world, men and women. It seemed as if it was an endless line. And then there were the many friends and family from Philadelphia and beyond who gathered to share this moment with me. There was glorious music, brass fanfares, choirs from churches large and small, young people and old. I sat, as is the custom, in the midst of the congregation the people who had elected me bishop suffragan of Massachusetts and I would, at the right moment and in response to their call expressed through the presiding bishop of the Episcopal Church, rise out of them to accept responsibility and authority for and with them.

The music was especially significant for me. I chose most of it, selecting things that had meaning in my life. I did have to give up one hymn that several women on the consecration committee thought was sexist.

Oh praise ye the Lord! Praise him in the height;
rejoice in his word, ye angel of light
ye heavens adore him by whom ye were made
and worship before him in brightness arrayed.

The Hymnal 1982, page 432

While I certainly support inclusive language, admittedly it was not one of my priorities. Some women, for example, have difficulty with the hymn "Rise Up, O Men of God." Most African Americans, with a different cultural perspective, do not. For us it's a call to the brothers to join us in the struggle. Perhaps it is our peculiar sensitivity to the needs of black men who, in our society, continue to be oppressed. Similarly, as a race which has had kingships stolen from us, we have no problem with "King of kings and Lord of lords," or with Jesus Christ as "sovereign."

In fact, as the procession of which I was a part—one of four—entered the hall, the massed choirs of St. Pauls' African Methodist Episcopal Church in Cambridge, Massachusetts were belting out "Ride on King Jesus, No man can a-hinder me," interspersed with the strains of "In that great gittin' up mornin'." I remember turning to one of my attending presbyters (priests) and remarking: "What a hell of a welcome!"

I also inserted a hymn to come after Paul Washington's rousing sermon—a little unusual in an Episcopal consecration liturgy. But "Close to Thee" was one of my grandmother's favorites and I wanted it sung, gospel style, by the choir of St. Paul's AME Church to convey to those present the basis and tone of my episcopacy. For those who did not hear it, the written words alone can scarcely convey the depth and power of the great old song:

Thou my everlasting portion,
More than friend or life to me,
All along my pilgrim journey,
Savior, let me walk with Thee.
Not for ease or worldly pleasure,
Nor for fame my prayer shall be;
Gladly will I toil and suffer,
Only let me walk with Thee.

"Close to Thee," Frances J. Crosby

As I mentioned earlier, I sat there for the objections that were to come as the presiding bishop then said, according to the Book of Common Prayer, ". . . the following, or similar words, and ask[ed] the response of the people":

Brothers and sisters in Christ Jesus, you have heard the testimony given that (name) has been duly and lawfully elected to be a bishop of the Church of God to serve in the Diocese of N. You have been assured of this suitability and that the Church has approved him for this sacred responsibility. Nevertheless, if any of you know any reason why we should not proceed let it now be known.

While I wondered if the objections would be personal, I was reasonably confident that Bishop Browning would deal with them handily.

Would the objections, for example, refer to my lack of a college or seminary degree? It had never been made clear that while working full time in the field of public relations, I had taken almost the equivalent number of courses in various institutions around Philadelphia and in England but the numbers had never added up in any one place to satisfy degree requirements, or included work that had been taken in non-degree granting places of study. Oxford-educated former presiding bishop, Frank T. Griswold also does not hold a seminary degree. But, as he says: "Nobody mentions that."

The education issue was a source of irritation for me. I had broad educational experiences including the executive management program at Penn State University, two years of pastoral care and counseling education, and many other courses that stood me in pretty good stead. So I resented the inferences that I was functionally illiterate. Interestingly, since that time I have received fourteen honorary doctorates from leading colleges, universities, and theological schools, including Yale University.

I must say, however, that my first honorary degree—Doctor of Sacred Theology—awarded by Hobart and William Smith Colleges in Geneva, New York at its 1981 commencement, is highly prized because it was bestowed when I was a "nobody." And that year, at the request of the students whom I had encountered while serving as a visiting fellow for the Association of Episcopal Colleges, I was invited to be the baccalaureate preacher.

The objections might also center around my mere nine years of ordination as a priest, my very short, ill-fated marriage and divorce many, many years before, or my minimal parish experience. Who knew what would be said?

I was well aware that some detractors were almost violent in their opposition. In fact, the Boston Police Department had offered me a bullet-proof vest, which I refused, figuring that if some fool was crazy enough to shoot me there was no better place to go than at the altar of God, surrounded by eight thousand five hundred of my closest friends.

So to say the least, I was nervous sitting there. But as the detractors began to drone on, not, as it turned out, about anything to do with me particularly, but to the canonical or legal situation surrounding my consecration, principally holding that the Episcopal Church had never by constitutional change specifically approved of the ordination of women to anything. Interestingly, two of the objections at my consecration were proffered at the Washington National Cathedral when the late Jane Holmes Dixon became the second woman bishop in the country and one when Mary Adelia McLeod became the third (and the first woman diocesan bishop), which was in Vermont. It also should be noted that the short speeches offered in opposition to the consecrations were pretty poor in quality and I was embarrassed for a young woman from Massachusetts who spoke at the Vermont service. She sounded like an ill-prepared seventh grader.

Given the nature of these objections when given at my consecration I began to worry even more about something else, that is, the woman sitting across the aisle from me—my mother.

As I mentioned earlier, mom had originally been opposed to the ordination of women but had been convinced of its correctness over the years, at least partially by the fact of the numbers of her friends who showed up for my ordination as a deacon. By the time I was ordained priest, a year later, she had become one of my strongest supporters.

All these images were pressing on my mind that day in the Hynes Auditorium. I was hoping my mother would not attack my objectors. Suddenly I was aware that someone was standing beside me. It was, in fact, my mother. She took my wrist in her hand, looked straight into my face and said quietly to me, "Have no fear. God is on our side. Everything is going to be all right." Then she stared into my eyes and said, "This is your momma." She turned and went back to her seat.

My sister didn't get up, but she looked across and mouthed, "Are you all right?" I nodded and blew her a kiss. It had been her idea to give me a charm bracelet one year with the inscription, "From your Yo Yos," meaning "yo' momma and yo' sister" so I knew what she meant.

The consecration brought some other unexpected support from some other unusual places. While the objections were going on, there was a loud shout from the balcony, "Go home!" which brought laughter into a tense moment. However the presiding bishop felt he had to admonish the crowd, "Please give the courtesy of the microphone to the speaker." Weeks later a young man came up to me as I was crossing the campus of the Episcopal Divinity School in Cambridge to announce "Hi, I'm Fred." When I failed to place him, he informed me that he had attended the consecration with a friend, a Roman Catholic priest who supported women's ordination, and he was the one who had yelled out the suggestion to the objectors. "Oh," I said, "that Fred." Strange and unexpected support indeed.

Following the two impassioned pleas not to continue with a "pretended consecration," Bishop Browning stated firmly that the objections raised had been widely vented in previous months, but nevertheless a majority of standing committees and a majority of bishops having jurisdiction had consented to the election. Then he uttered the magic words: "Under these circumstances, we will proceed with the consecration of the candidate as printed in your programs." The applause was thunderous. He then asked, as specified by the Prayer Book: "Is it your will that we ordain Barbara a bishop?" The response shook the rafters and caused him and the entire assembly to pause and then burst into joyous laughter.

But perhaps the best response to the objections came from Paul Washington, with the sermon that followed. Paul delivered a stirring sermon in which he ventured to say that my election and consecration were pre-ordained. He drew a parallel to the prophet Jeremiah, daring to quote: "before I formed you in the womb I knew you and before you were born I consecrated you . . ." I don't know how others heard these words, but they gave me tremendous pause and I felt that a great responsibility had been laid on me.

He went on to paraphrase the apostle Paul saying: "Today God has chosen the foolish thing of the world to confound the wise. He has chosen the weak thing of the world to confound the mighty and one who has been at the base of our society, despised, a nobody, to bring to naught things that are." My own interpretation was that this put those who opposed my election and consecration on notice that they were not the final arbiters of how or by whom God can be served.

All of this took place, I might add, in the presence of the governor of Massachusetts and the mayor of Boston, who were among the many civic and ecumenical dignitaries present. And speaking of dignitaries, the initial chairperson of my consecration committee wanted to invite then-President George H. W. Bush. I asked why. The next thing I knew he had resigned from the committee.

There was also a round of luncheons and receptions which did not allow much time for quiet reflection on the morning of the event. It was not until late that night that I had an opportunity to sit quietly with my family and try to put into perspective what had taken place earlier in the day. That night I thought about the moments that brought laughter, for even though it was a stressful and a somewhat frightening time, there were some funny moments—even during the service.

In the midst of the service there was an incident which was videotaped and photographed and which many people have seen. The bishops had laid their hands on me and I was being vested according to my new office as a bishop as the service requires. We came to the miter, that ridiculously funny pointed hat that bishops wear, which was handed to me. Mine had been made, along with my other vestments for that day, by Challwood Studios in New York and was trimmed in richly colored Ghanaian women's weave kente cloth. It bore the Ashanti inscription *NYame Nwu Na M'awu*, meaning, "Could God die, I would die," thus expressing God's eternity and creation's dependence. I wasn't sure if I or someone else was to place it on my head, so I asked the presiding bishop. He said, "Yeah, go for it." I put it on, the crowd roared, and I guess in sheer delight and nervousness, I opened my mouth and stuck out my tongue. Bishop Browning howled with laughter and the crowd cheered.

There was another moment after the consecration itself when I spotted some people from Church of the Advocate for the first time. I started waving to them, the Chinese choir was singing behind us and Bishop Browning was twisted around in his chair to listen to them, and various people were walking around the platform. He turned to me and said, "You know, there's just too much going on here."

There was a lot going on in addition to the service. People around the country were either celebrating or lamenting what was taking place. As regards the latter, one parish in Philadelphia—which for years has been embroiled in dispute with the diocese—held a requiem because the bishop of Pennsylvania was one of my co-consecrators. The parish rector was reported to have said, "The See is vacant and the diocese is dead." My being referred to as the "final crisis" was a bit much for my mother who asked me, "How can one little, skinny, nappy-haired black woman stand this church on its ear?"

Following the service there was a huge press conference at which the question was put to me several times, "What do you have to say to your detractors?" My response was that there was really nothing for me to say. The church had spoken and over eight thousand assembled clergy and laity and sixty plus bishops did not represent the lunatic fringe of the Episcopal world.

The Unexpected

"We just cannot elect her."

Douglas: *Now tell me this, you talked about being surprised at all the people that came and recognizing on that morning that whoa you're stepping into history, were you surprised? Were you surprised at the reaction of the world, the media, etc. to your election?*

Harris: *Well, yes and no. I was surprised in some ways that people would try to dig at negative stuff in my life.*

Douglas: *What were you scared that they would find?*

Harris: *I think I, not that what I was scared they would find, but that they would attack the education. That I was ill-prepared and as I said Frank Griswold said he never went to seminary* *but no one said anything. Of course that he was trained at Oxford makes a difference. But, that they, people just, I mean, they tried, you know, to dig at age and the fact that I was single, divorced rather. Not so much single, but divorced. I don't know if I ever told you this, people called 815 and said well she's divorced and they said yes and they said well what is her sexual preference?*

Douglas: *They asked that?*

Harris: *Mmm-hmm. And when I found out about that I said I wished they had called me directly, I would have told them that you don't always get your preference, but mine would be for several times a week.*

Douglas: *How did the black Episcopal priests, that is males, respond to your election? Were there any surprises, were they supportive? Because I know there were many that were not.*

Harris: *One of the well-respected black male priests who was rector of a parish in DC for many years said it was ludicrous.*

Douglas: *Oh he told you that?*

Harris: *He didn't tell me, he was overheard saying that it was ludicrous.*

As I look back over my life I marvel at the number of times I have received unexpected, sometimes even undeserved, support. The most striking occasion of unexpected support in fact came during the time of my consecration process, even among those who opposed. For example, the one-time bishop of Northern Indiana told me, "I was totally opposed to your consecration, but I want you to know that I think you have conducted yourself with much more grace than some of your detractors and I hope one day we can become friends." We did, over the years, develop great respect for each other, having worked closely together on a nominating committee for the presiding bishop election of 1997.

Similarly, a now-retired priest of the diocese confided that as the balloting for my election proceeded, he was among those who said, "We just cannot elect *her*," and joined the group that caucused to try to garner the necessary votes for my closest contender. Today I count him as a close personal friend who thinks the diocese made the right choice.

The unexpected support continued. I remember a white woman who lived in a section of Boston from which you wouldn't expect a person to come forward with support. This woman said to me soon after I moved to Boston, "I know what it means to leave home and family and come to a new place, starting a new work. If you ever need a mother, you have one here."

And there was the elderly man on Cape Cod who said, "Baby, you just keep on doing what you're doing." His wife was horrified and said to him, "You don't call a bishop, 'baby!'" He looked me right in the eye and said, "She knows what I mean." And a gentleman somewhere in Texas melted down all of his gold and fashioned it into a large handsome cross which he sent me with a wonderful note. Unfortunately, he did not provide a return address and I never was able to express my deep appreciation for such a thoughtful and generous offering. These expressions of confidence from wonderful ordinary people meant as much to me as the words of famous theologians and powerful ecclesiastics.

In fact, the first letter of congratulations I received was from the Rev. Robert Schuler of the Crystal Cathedral in California. It was a very warm and lovely letter of support. I can't imagine how he even knew about the consecration or why he cared so much, but it was an unexpected and delightful surprise.

After the consecration, when the time came for me to attend my first House of Bishops meeting in Philadelphia, Roger Blanchard, the retired Bishop of Southern Ohio, organized five retired bishops who lived in Massachusetts and drove them down to that meeting. Most retired bishops don't regularly attend those gatherings, but Roger figured it would be helpful for me to see those men, whom I had gotten to know, there for me. I think he also thought it might be helpful for their colleagues in the House of Bishops to see how firmly they were behind me. They didn't stay long, just long enough to show the flag and let me and the House know they cared.

There have been so many others whose strong support and influence on my ministry must be acknowledged, not the least of whom are most of the men and their spouses who made up my "class" of "baby bishops"—those consecrated the same year I was or shortly before. The bishops of Province I (the seven dioceses of New England) welcomed me into their midst even before the consent process had been completed. My mentor in the House of Bishops, the late John Thomas Walker, then bishop of Washington, DC, and one of my co-consecrators, brought me to the Washington National Cathedral to preach and to concelebrate with him early on in my episcopate and wrote how glad he was that we had the opportunity to share such precious time. I remember shortly after his consecration we stood next to each other at a celebration of the Eucharist during an annual meeting of the Union of Black Episcopalians. We were singing "Lean on Me," and he turned toward me and said, "I will be leaning on you." When I asked him to be my mentor I could not believe that he told me that no one had ever before asked him to fill that role.

My subsequent mentor in the House, H. Coleman McGehee, then-retired bishop of Michigan—with whom I had served on the board of the Episcopal Church Publishing Company years earlier—enthusiastically assumed Bishop Walker's tutelage. The bishops of Pennsylvania, active and retired bishops such as Antonio Ramos, the late Paul Moore, along with former presiding bishops Edmond Browning and the late John Elbridge Hines all rallied round and their comments to me are stored as treasure in my heart. There also have been countless clergy, male and female, and scores of lay women and men in such organizations as the Union of Black Episcopalians, the Episcopal Women's Caucus and The Consultation, a coalition of progressive groups with the church. I cannot say enough about them and without them the journey and the struggle would have been infinitely more difficult if not impossible.

I fondly remember "Petey" Reid, a resident of Martha's Vineyard who dubbed herself "unofficial bishop's aide" and who, among other things created for me a needlepoint prayer cushion emblazoned with the diocesan seal, my initials and the date of my consecration. I still use it. She also initiated a long-running, almost weekly correspondence friendship with my mother, whom she never met. And until her demise, also from the Vineyard, my mailbox yielded an occasional note of encouragement penned by Mrs. Esther Burgess, another resident of the Vineyard, stalwart defender of truth, and wife of Massachusetts' first black bishop, John Melville Burgess, who was bishop diocesan from 1970 to 1975. Also, there have been particular colleagues in ministry who took loving care of me, including the late Reverend Joseph A. Pelham, who served so admirably as executive director of the Episcopal City Mission in the Diocese of Massachusetts and many who continue to do so. These include the Rev. Nan Peete, all my ROPE sisters (the former Black Women's Task Force) who presented me with my pectoral cross and who all have small replicas of it, and two former members of the diocesan staff—the Rev. Randall Chase, and the Rev. Canon Edward Rodman, who has written the forward to this book and has kept me out of more trouble than I could even imagine.

As I think of those who consistently encouraged my ministry over the years, Van Bird and Paul Washington, whom I mentioned earlier, loom large. Both were with me through my whole process of discernment, preparation and ordination, preached me into the diaconate, the priesthood, and the episcopate, respectively and who perhaps saw my election from a different perspective than others. Both men always regarded me as a work in progress, in whose development they had a strong vested interest.

In the midst of the plaudits and brickbats, strong and some weak-kneed supporters and cordial opponents, stood my mother, my family, and my oldest and dearest friends. They have carried me through many a dark time and difficult passages. My mother especially had always been on hand when I needed her most. While the timing and nature of her support on the day of my consecration were not exactly expected, my mother was a strong ally all through her life.

As I indicated earlier, as I was walking into that auditorium on that Saturday morning in February toward my consecration, a number of thoughts were running through my mind. But all in all, I was in a good place by the time I came forward for my examination and actual consecration and I was able to answer the questions of the examining bishops with confidence and conviction.

The Day After

"Forget the ring, sweetie, kiss the bishop."

The following day was equally crowded. My first duty was to preach in the cathedral. The church was packed when I arrived, and I was busy greeting friends from around the country who had stayed over for the Sunday morning service. I was somewhat oblivious to members of the media following me and when a male friend from Maryland called out, "Barbara let me kiss your ring, I have never kissed a bishop's ring," I shouted back, "Forget the ring, sweetie, kiss the bishop." My response was picked up by a Los Angeles newspaper.

From the cathedral I went on to visit with and bless the unborn children of some pregnant teenage residents of Crittenden House, a shelter and educational center for young unwed mothers. Again, the press was in hot pursuit, but I insisted that the visit with the young women was private and the media was kept at bay until we emerged for punch and cookies under the glare of flashbulbs.

That afternoon at historic St. Bartholomew's Church, the Massachusetts chapter of the Union of Black Episcopalians held its annual service honoring Absalom Jones, the first African American priest in the Episcopal Church. Even as I tried to rest before the service, I was being interviewed by a national black magazine which ran a most inelegant photo of me with my unshod feet propped unceremoniously up in a chair.

CHAPTER SIX

Lord Make Me a Blessing

uring the 1904 and 1907 General Conventions, debate ensued over the Suffragan Plan. This plan was a part of a wider discussion surrounding the "expediency" of black leadership within the Episcopal Church in America. This plan allowed for black men to be made bishops, but only under the supervision of white diocesans. Moreover, they would only be permitted to supervise black members of the church and they would not have a vote in the House of Bishops or be able to automatically succeed the diocesan bishop. This plan was adopted in 1907. In 1918 the first black bishops were consecrated under this plan. They were Bishop Thomas Demby (Arkansas) and Bishop Henry Delaney (North Carolina). For many they were bishops in name only. They would remain the only black suffragans until 1962 when John Burgess was consecrated suffragan of Massachusetts, later to be the first black diocesan bishop in 1969. It was fitting, therefore, that the diocese of Massachusetts would elect the first female bishop and that she would be black. That she was suffragan was also fitting, as there were those with whom Bishop Harris served that considered her bishop in "name only." This chapter tells that story.

After the consecration and all the excitement, I went to work for the diocese. One of the first things requested of me was to hand over a sizable chunk of money from my discretionary fund to help pay for my underbudgeted consecration. It was then that I also learned what a ridiculously low salary I was to be paid. Ironically, I had taken a cut in pay to ascend to one of the highest offices in the church.

Doing the Work of Bishop

"I don't want your help."

I never really clicked with Bishop David Johnson. I spent almost six years working with him but he didn't seem to want much help from me. He put me in charge of the cathedral which meant I wasn't out in the diocese making visitations two Sundays a month. But this was all right because the cathedral congregation suddenly felt cared for, which had not been true before. I was closer to one of our assisting bishops, David Birney, as I continued to feel disconnected from David Johnson.

Douglas: *And so how did Bishop Johnson make life for you during your time with him?*

Harris: *Well, he tried to in some ways cut me off from the diocese. He asked me, well one thing, he brought in an assisting bishop and I learned about this at the consecration. Following the laying on of hands, David went to the microphone, asked me to join him at the microphone, and then asked Bishop David Birney, who had been the bishop of Iowa, to join us and announced this is what the diocese of Massachusetts is going to look like for the next little while. And that was my first knowledge that he had asked David Birney to be assisting bishop.*

Douglas: *What were your thoughts when that announcement got made?*

Harris: *I thought to myself, you don't want to work with me all by yourself, that's why you've done this. And on another occasion, in a conversation with David, I said something about why don't you let me help with that and he said, "I don't want your help."*

Douglas: *Really?*

Harris: *Mmhmm, he said, "I don't want your help." And that's when I really knew he didn't want me there.*

Douglas: *How did David Birney treat you? How did you all interact?*

Harris: *We developed a great relationship. He treated me with respect and shared some of the wisdom of his years as a bishop and consulted my opinion on things. And in fact I learned when he died that he had specifically requested that I conduct his funeral and deliver his eulogy and I didn't know it until that time. He was in Kentucky, in retirement.*

Douglas: *Did you deliver the eulogy?*

Harris: *Yes, and I presided at the funeral and I didn't know until I got to Kentucky that he had wanted me to preside. And of course the bishop of the diocese was present. And I said I hope you're not uncomfortable with this. And I said why don't we concelebrate.*

Honey, given who that bishop was at the time, all I can say is God has got one sense of humor. He said ok. I don't think he was that comfortable but he did it.

David Johnson also had a way of letting his true feelings slip out. On one occasion he told a congregation that we would make an interesting team with my "ghetto background" and his "middle-class upbringing." Since he knew little or nothing of my background, his assumption not only struck me as curious, it ticked me off. So I did my thing, went around, tried to preach the gospel and love people. The response was warm and welcoming in most places. Where I knew I wasn't welcome, I didn't go. I had enough to do without going where I wasn't wanted. I had enough of that in my life. On the other hand, even though one rector in the diocese was very opposed to women's ordination, he always was very cordial. When I addressed a convocation at one of the state colleges he appeared, the only clergy person in his area to do so. He earned my respect though I never visited his congregation. There are only three parishes in the diocese where I never celebrated the Eucharist, two of which I never visited.

Navigating Gender

"You can go now."

My first visitation was to Trinity Church in the city of Boston, our largest and most affluent urban parish where I confirmed, received, and reaffirmed large numbers of people. The rector at the time, whose less-than-substantive sermons were delivered in stentorian tones, was very patronizing and I felt a coldness. I was introduced to the clergy staff as they enjoyed coffee from china cups as I was given tea in a Styrofoam vessel. In fact, after the service and the coffee hour, during which I was told exactly where to stand on a lavish oriental carpet, he told me "You can go now," which was remarkably ungracious.

My journal entry from that day reads:

> First visitation today—Trinity, Copley Square. Perhaps thought by some to be the jewel of the diocese. It is marked by a "genteel arrogance," which makes for polite put-downs— manifested in several subtle ways, typical of so many Episcopal clergy and congregations. Trinity has the money to back it up.
>
> First visitation: 74 confirmations, 21 receptions. Rite I service. The spirit of E. Sydnor Thomas was present, hovering over me like a protective cloud and enabling me to celebrate almost from memory. ("Let the fiery, cloud pillar lead me all my journey through.") Gave a head sermon versus heart sermon. Lord don't let me fall into intellectualism in the pulpit. That's not me!

That same day I went to a tiny city parish nearby, St. Stephen's, where the welcome was warm and overwhelming and where I confirmed four little black and Latina girls. The contrast was interesting, especially in the great feeling of satisfaction I had being with the struggling people of that poor parish.

Again, my journal entry reflects that difference in the two visitations.

Afternoon—St. Stephen's in the south end. What contrast, what spirit, what joy. Confirmation four young black and Hispanic girls. Truly bilingual worship—not forced. Spirited worship felt like home (Advocate). Hope I can find this from time to time in other places. Would help to ease the transition and the longing for home.

Truly A Bishop

"You look like you have been doing this all your life."

Even though I had a few butterflies in my stomach when I began as a bishop, relatively early on it began to feel natural. I took my first ordination in Poughkeepsie, New York. The young ordinand had specifically requested that I ordain him and Bishop Paul Moore Jr., an old friend and strong supporter, graciously gave permission. At least one priest in the New York diocese objected to my being the ordaining bishop, complaining that Paul Moore should have done it himself or, at the very least, have the young man come to Massachusetts. I drove over for the service with one of my dear clergy friends. All went well and he said, "You look like you have been doing this all your life."

Douglas: *Before we move on to talk about your experiences in the House of Bishops, tell me about your relationship with Tom Shaw.*

Harris: *We were close, close friends.*

Harris: *When Tom was elected co-adjutor, David Johnson said to him, "You oughta get rid of Barbara Harris."*

Douglas: *Really? On what grounds? How is he gonna do that?*

Harris: *He said, "She doesn't do anything for the diocese."*

Douglas: *And what did Tom Shaw, obviously he told you that.*

Harris: *He said, "David said I should get rid of you, that you don't do anything, that you don't do anything for the diocese."*

Douglas: *How did that make you feel?*

Harris: *I thought to myself, I've done more in my little time here for this diocese than you have.*

Tom Shaw was elected coadjutor in 1994. Soon after that, David Johnson committed suicide after he learned that his sexual indiscretions were about to be made public. Bishop Shaw and I had a genuine friendship, which continued to his death. We loved each other in the best sense of that word. Tom shared leadership easily and was not concerned to concentrate power in his own hands. Beyond that, he was really smart, intellectually very able. We had a precious conversation every Sunday night when we shared the happenings of the day and what was going on.

Tom introduced me to his monastic order, the Society of St. John the Evangelist, and I love having dinner with them at Easter, Thanksgiving and on other occasions. They've been a real family for me these past few years.

House of Bishops

"it's easy to ignore one, two or even three women sitting in that body, but . . ."

Douglas: *How did it feel being the only woman sitting in the House of Bishops?*

Harris: *Well, it was strange but interesting. What happened was, my first meeting of the House was in Philadelphia and I had been to meetings of the House before when I worked for the Episcopal Church Publishing Company and the bishops always had their business sessions separately; spouses came in for social events or maybe one joint forum or something. I got to Philadelphia and they decided to have the spouses sit in on the whole House of Bishops meeting. So I got lost in a sea of spouses. That was my first House meeting.*

Douglas: *And what did you do? How did you respond to that?*

Harris: *Well, a resolution came up and people went to the microphone to speak for or against it and I wanted, I spoke for the resolution and the bishop behind me, when I finished, jumped to the microphone and immediately spoke against it without the presiding bishop ever dealing with what I said. So when he finished I went back to the microphone and I said, my resolution was not dealt with by the chair. And so then they had to deal with it. It probably was defeated, but still I wanted it at least dealt with. And they used to have separate Bible studies. In Philadelphia, they lumped you in groups and the spouses were in the Bible study groups which had never happened before.*

Douglas: *You're kidding*

Harris: *I kid you not. And then there was some committee that was in the House that wanted to, had to deal with how people were responding to my consecration, following the consecration. They interviewed one or two conservative bishops but they never interviewed me.*

Douglas: *Now why did they have a committee to see how people were responding to you?*

Harris: *I don't remember. I have to go back and look. That's in Pam Darling's book, New Wine. Yeah, I'll have to look that up in Pam Darling's book. But they never talked to me. I guess it was people were responding to my presence. The most memorable thing about the 1991 General Convention it was the last time the House of Bishops sat in order of consecration. The most memorable thing about that General Convention in Phoenix was that I had a whole ladies room to myself. Fourteen stalls, no waiting.*

I'd been at the House of Bishops before as an observer for the Episcopal Church Publishing Company and I knew many of the bishops, so it seemed natural to sit there among them. It's easy to be ignored as one woman and also as three, and some bishops did just that—ignore me. But now there are many more of us and as the number has grown, the atmosphere has gradually changed. We no longer sit in order of consecration, rather at round tables or in small groups. So in almost any direction you look you see a woman and that makes things different. At the risk of taking too much credit, I think we also have brought a candor to the discussions that was not there before.

I don't wish to imply that it's all been easy. The objections continued through the first three ordinations of women bishops here in the United States, sometimes in ways that seemed transparently manipulative. When Jane Holmes Dixon was consecrated in Washington, DC, the objectors were both disabled persons who had to be helped down the aisle by a verger of the cathedral. To me it was shameful to use people that way. And when Mary Adelia McLeod of the diocese of Vermont was consecrated in 1993, the objector was a young woman, who I mentioned earlier, gave a very immature and poorly prepared speech. This was about a seventh grade level discourse by a young woman from a parish in the diocese of Massachusetts. She was backed up by a silent beefy woman from Washington, DC. The latter was also a staunch supporter of a black priest adamantly opposed to the ordination of women. I remember wishing the objectors would do a better job of presenting their case and not embarrassing us and the people for whom they were speaking.

Women have also settled into the House of Bishops. As I've said, it's easy to ignore one, two or even three women sitting in that body, but as our numbers have increased and as we have become increasingly comfortable, we have become increasingly difficult to ignore. There was pressure, of course, pressure to blend in, to avoid taking uncomfortable or awkward oppositional stands. This has affected some of our women clergy as well, especially younger ones who did not have to struggle to be ordained. I think we will hear fewer strident female voices in the House, particularly as some of us retire. I regret that.

I so valued my friendship with the late Jane Dixon. When I began writing this, Jane had been designated bishop pro tem, or acting bishop, and was going through a particularly tough time in refusing to accept a priest as rector of a parish whose expressed agenda was to lead parishes out of the Episcopal Church. I applauded her stand. I know of no male bishops who would have a priest in their diocese who refused to accept their ecclesiastical authority. Once again, those who criticized her obscured the issue, pretending she opposed the priest because he opposed ordination of women. That was not the issue. The issue was his refusal to accept her authority and his attempt to sever the parish from the Church. Any bishop worth his or her salt would have done as Jane did.

You have to deal with the politics always, even, or maybe especially in the House of Bishops, given the increasing frenzy of the radical right within the Episcopal Church—they refer to themselves as "traditionalists." For example, Jane, Mary Adelia, and I did organize a little revolt in the House some years ago over a resolution, the content of which now eludes me. We organized "Teams A, B, and C" to demand a roll call vote on the resolution and the subsequent amendment and substitute resolution we knew were to follow. We were determined to smoke out people and not let them hide behind a simple voice vote. We defeated the matter before the third vote. You have to be ready to do that kind of thing. It's easy to forget that our opponents on many issues of justice are very well organized so it is well to heed the biblical admonition to be as wise as serpents and as innocent as doves.

Disappointing Moments with Women Bishops

"They're just not supportive."

Douglas: *You have mentioned to me before some of your disappointments with the women that have followed you.*

Harris: *Yeah, they're just not supportive of . . .*

Douglas: *Such as?*

Harris: *Jane Dixon's funeral occurred between Christmas and New Year's.*

Douglas: *And women weren't there for that?*

Harris: *Right. And at Marianne Budde's consecration, there were only three retired women bishops present. Yes, me and Chilton Knutson, were the only other woman. Mary Glasspool was a co-consecrator, but, and I guess maybe that woman from Southern Virginia, Susan Goff, may have been there, but the rest of the women bishops were not, none of them were present, and I thought Marianne's consecration was important given that it was the Diocese of Washington DC.*

Douglas: *Right, right. Do you know about how many women bishops there are?*

Harris: *Twenty. Maybe twenty-two?*

Sexuality and Matters of Justice/Matters of Unity

"At times it is as difficult to fathom what holds the Anglican Communion together beyond our love of the Lord Jesus Christ and Wippell's."

While some people think it's beating a dead horse, I think it's necessary to speak of justice all the time, to keep those issues in our consciousness, otherwise the issues of racism, poverty, gender inequality, and so forth, disappear from our minds. They make us uncomfortable and above all, we want to be comfortable. This denial might be natural, but we have to resist it.

One of the church-related groups that keep issues of justice alive is the Episcopal Women's Caucus, which has honored me in several ways. They invited me to speak at their breakfast during the General Convention in Denver in 2000. They renamed their special projects fund the Barbara C. Harris Leadership Fund and they granted me a life membership.

This wonderful group of women took very good care of the women bishops at the Lambeth Conference 1998 doing whatever needed to be done—errands, mailings, shopping, any and everything supportive. They also held a daily vigil under the trees with the Women's Watch organization from England that I was privileged to join from time to time.

So much has been said about Lambeth 1998, especially about the controversy over homosexuality that I hesitate to go into again. Beyond that, it was in many ways a painful and arduous experience and it took a while to put it in perspective. The clash of cultures was extreme and complicated. For example, when the bishops of Papua, New Guinea led a Eucharist in what amounted to Pidgin English, I was astonished by the opening sentence which rendered the familiar "Father, Son, and Holy Spirit" into "The Papa, the Pikinnini and the Holi Spirit." After I picked myself off the ground I realized that *Pikininni* is indigenous to their native tongue. As I said in an article in the diocesan newspaper following the decennial gathering, "At times it is as difficult to fathom what holds the Anglican Communion together beyond our love of the Lord Jesus Christ and Wippell's [the international outfitters to the clergy]."

At Lambeth we were jolted by a very different approach to the interpretation of scripture. In addition, our American democratic spirit of sharing authority expressed in the relationship of clergy and laity was challenged by an understanding of episcopacy which gives absolute authority to diocesan bishops.

As I wrote at the time:

On reflection it was also clear that Lambeth 1998 had brought some Anglican "chickens home to roost." The vitriolic, fundamentalist rhetoric of African, Asian and other bishops of color—who were in the majority—was reflective of the European and North American missionary influence propounded in Southern Hemisphere nations during the eighteenth, nineteenth and early twentieth centuries. In truth, none of us should have been surprised by their hardline stance on gays and lesbians and the role of women in the church, rooted as it was in a belief in the inerrancy and primacy of scripture, which support a preexisting cultural bias. Thus they brought to Lambeth the same "truth" that not only had been handed to their forbearers, but had been used to suppress them.

This fundamentalist approach fit perfectly with the aspirations of a small contingent of US bishops who had been unable to move their agenda at the previous summer's General Convention of the church in Philadelphia. There were allegations of "dirty tricks" as the conservative lobby was accused of running a "spin-doctor service" for bishops friendly to their interests. Particularly dismaying were reports of cash gifts, and the use of pagers and mobile phones to call a central headquarters near the campus that provided points of instant rebuttal for use in the debate. The bishop of Edinburgh and primus of the Church in Scotland further accused the lobbying group of trying to win the hearts and minds of the Africans and Asians with "chicken and sausages,"—a pointed reference to the several barbecue receptions which they hosted.

Perhaps the most disappointing was what many felt to be a lack of leadership by the president of the conference, the archbishop of Canterbury. His statements to the plenary sessions, particularly the one just prior to the vote on the sexuality resolution, seemed sadly lacking substance and vision. By contrast, the leadership of the Spouse's Programme by the archbishop's wife was decisive, powerful and grace-filled.

I also observed that "grace-filled" could be used to describe the warm reception accorded to the eleven women bishops attending the Lambeth Conference for the first time in its history. We were, indeed, treated with courtesy and respect and the open hostility reported prior to the conference was not in evidence, at least not on the surface. Some of us were asked to fill responsible roles at the conference. I served as moderator of my subsection on "Visible Unity and Ethical Witness." Those opposed to our presence simply seemed to avoid us.

The other shoe dropped, however, in the plenary discussion of a resolution titled "Unity of the Anglican Communion." Two women bishops got coopted, and in a series of secret meetings with "traditionalist" bishops, helped to hammer out the odious amendment—clearly directed at the American church— approving freedom of conscience on women's ordination and "flying bishops"—the practice of bringing in a male bishop to exercise episcopal acts where there might be opposition to the diocesan bishop, especially if that bishop is a woman. Fortunately, the non-binding nature of Lambeth resolutions has no real effect on the canons and polity of the church here or in any other province where local policies take precedence.

This appeal became blatantly apparent during the 2003 General Convention debate on the approval of the Rev. Canon V. Gene Robinson as bishop coadjutor of the Diocese of New Hampshire. Despite some last minute patently transparent dirty tricks to discredit him as bishop-elect, he was confirmed by a more than respectable majority in both the House of Deputies and the House of Bishops. Thus the church acknowledged that gays and lesbians not only are a significant part of our culture, they are a significant and active presence in our church as both lay and ordained persons.

Interestingly, bishops from other provinces of the Communion which today are most vocal in their criticism of the American church on the whole issue of human sexuality—of which women's ordination is a part—told the Lambeth Conference of 1988 that they should be left alone to deal with aspects of life in their countries which were reflective of their culture, such as polygamy. They, however, do not adhere to the same discipline on the matter of homosexuality.

But even more interesting is the perpetration of the myth by some US bishops and their adherents that Canon Gene

Robinson represented the first "openly" gay bishop in the Episcopal Church. He may have been the first, prior to conse-cration, who acknowledged that he had or lived with a same-sex partner of many years, but God knows, as do many of us, there are gay men—active and inactive—who have been mem-bers of the House of Bishops for some time. Truth be told, "Don't ask, don't tell" was the byword in that body, just as it was in the military.

It was the 1979 convention which considered a resolution which said ". . . we do not feel it appropriate to ordain homo-sexuals or heterosexuals involved in sex outside of marriage." I was a first-time deputy that year but I jumped up and amended that language with the insertion of two simple words, so that the resolution would read . . . "We *no longer* feel it is appro-priate. . . ." A gasp went down the center of the room and someone yelped, "I don't believe she said that." All I was try-ing to do was to get us to acknowledge that ordination of gay people was not a new phenomenon and it was disingenuous, at best, if not outright lying, to pretend otherwise.

Following that Lambeth Conference, Bishop Shaw and I hosted a group of "hot shot" bishops from other provinces of the Anglican Communion who were invited to "come and see," and tried to explain to them the ordination of gay and lesbian persons was not a new phenomenon. We said to them, "The genie has long been out of the bottle and it ain't going back in." I don't think we got much value out of all the time we spent on that, or, by the way, out of the expensive dinner we gave them.

I think we'll just have to agree to disagree over this one if we're going to move forward together in communion. I don't believe human sexuality is the issue over which to draw a line in the sand regarding the Anglican Communion. In a talk I gave to the Episcopal Women's Caucus on July 9, 2000, I said,

> And I'm like my Aunt Mae here, who prefaced everything she
> had to say with "and another thing again." So . . . another

thing again: I wonder if we are going to come and go from Denver with any clear appreciation of the issues we, as a church, ought to be addressing, such as world hunger, violence, international debt, distributive justice and the AIDS pandemic, or are we going to be mired in a post Lambeth "funk," perpetuated by a few bishops from the Southern Hemisphere, aided and abetted by a few from here, who do not understand or acknowledge our understanding of the authority and primacy of scripture and the inclusivity of the gospel?

I don't feel no ways tired, I come too far from where I started from.
Nobody told me that the road would be easy
I don't believe he brought me this far to leave me

—Calvin Burrell

Full Circle

Harris: *A few years ago, here it's coming full cycle, a few years ago I was on a visitation to a parish in the diocese, and I baptized the great-great grandson of the bishop who confirmed my mother in 1915.*

Douglas: *Whoa, how did that happen? Happenstance?*

Harris: *Yeah. Just happenstance. It wasn't planned. Just turned out that his name was Henry Rhinelander, and the bishop who confirmed my mother was Bishop Philip Rhinelander in 1915.*

Douglas: *And you remembered that?*

Harris: *Mmm-hmm.*

The True Pioneer

"I wonder what Pauli Murray would think today . . ."

Douglas: *Barbara, are there other moments during the course of your journey and ministry that stand out to you as you look back?*

Harris: *I didn't have much of a relationship with Pauli Murray. I knew who she was and I encountered her from time to time. But one encounter with her sticks out in my mind vividly. We were at a worship service in the cathedral in Newark, New Jersey and I don't remember what that service was at this time. But following the service we were at a reception in the parish hall and Pauli came to me and said, "why aren't you in seminary?" And I said, "I'm too old!" She said, "Too old!" and gave me the dressing down of my life. And it was then that I realized that she had indeed embarked on this third career at a point in her life where most people would have thought that it was ridiculous, that she was too old. But I will never forget the chastisement that she delivered to me that day about not ever being too old to do something, to begin something important in life. And, I had very few actual encounters with her following that but I will never forget that dressing down she gave me that day.*

Douglas: *Did you think of her at all, did she come to you at all during your ordination process or your consecration?*

Harris: *I think I did think about her when I was consecrated and thought I wonder what Pauli Murray would think today given her stellar life achievements.*

Douglas: *Were there any points that you were disappointed in yourself as you exercised your ministry as bishop?*

Harris: *Yes. I think there were times when I might have taken more forceful stands, particularly with the bishop of the diocese who really did not want me there.*

Douglas: *Do you feel there was anything left undone?*

Harris: *Well, yeah I guess I could have made, maybe, written some stuff while I was active, maybe made some more profound kind of statements, but by and large I think I acquitted myself well and probably beyond the expectations of (90% of the people) yeah some people.*

Douglas: *What's the thing you're proudest of as bishop, beyond that you think you did a good job, as you did?*

Harris: *I'm trying to think, I don't know that I . . . I think maybe . . . uh . . . the working relationship that I had with Tom Shaw. And, um, representing the church preaching at the World Council of Churches in Seoul, Korea in 1990. And then, spending nine days in the Diocese of Tokyo preaching so that they could be exposed to the ministry of a woman as they wrestled with how to bring about women's ordination in the church in Japan.*

Forgiving Dylann Roof

"I don't believe everything can be forgiven."

Douglas: *Barbara, before we go on can we go back to the idea of forgiveness? It strikes me that you said you would never forgive your rapist. Forgiveness, of course, became a topic in popular culture when the people of South Carolina forgave Dylann Roof. What are your thoughts on this?*

Harris: *I don't believe everything can be forgiven. Probably most things. But, I wonder sometimes when we say we forgive, if we are saying it to make ourselves look good as Christians. And do we really mean it, do we really forgive?*

Douglas: *Because what it means to forgive is not clear?*

Harris: *Yeah*

Douglas: *What's that mean to you, to forgive?*

Harris: *Not to erase it completely, nor to excuse it, but to say I am not going to allow this to influence or in any way direct what I do.*

Douglas: *One of the ways, Barbara that I thought about forgiveness, and have written about, the forgiveness of the people when they forgave Dylann Roof, was just that, forgiveness for them was not about exonerating Dylann Roof, not at all, but in fact what they were doing was freeing themselves from the sin that was Dylann Roof's, and freeing themselves from living in that cycle of hate, also freeing themselves from living in this cycle of despair where they knew that there would be no human justice that could ever make up for the loss of their loved ones and so they were able to forgive because they relied on the justice of God and so they released themselves from being trapped by Dylann Roof's vile sin. Of course, they also affirmed that God's love was greater than that white sin, or the sin of that white hate, so like you I believe that forgiveness for them was freeing, but that they freed themselves . . .*

Harris: *That's what I wanted to say. It's a freeing up of one's self so that you're not trapped in a cycle of hatred, resentment, and hurt. Or heartbreak.*

Douglas: *And I like the heartbreak part because if you think about what happened to a person, their heart is deeply broken and they can just stay in that despair and can't move on, or forgive so forgiveness is more about freeing yourself than it is about freeing the victimizer, so to speak.*

Harris: *Absolutely. Yeah, its freeing yourself from being trapped in a cycle of despair.*

Legacy of Humble Service

"Never get too big for your britches."

Douglas: *Was there ever a time during your time as bishop that you said, "Okay, this is where I'm supposed to be. It was supposed to be me."*

Harris: *No, I think I may have said to myself, "Okay, I'm here. And I am going to be the best that I can, especially in relating to people."*

Douglas: *Do you think that you gained the respect of your fellow bishops? Left or right wing?*

Harris: *Some of them. One bishop said to me, "I was totally opposed to your election and consecration but I think you're going to be a good bishop and I hope that we can be friends." And we served on the PB nominating committee together and I think we did become friends and he developed some respect for me.*

Douglas: *What are you thinking now as you look back on that?*

Harris: *I'm thinking, at least I didn't have illicit sex relations with clergy or somebody on the staff. And that I conducted myself appropriately. And that actually there were people in the diocese, clergy and laity, who had come to love and trust me.*

Douglas: *How long did it take you to build that?*

Harris: *I'm not sure. Some of it was manifested earlier than other pieces of it, but I think people responded to my genuinely caring what happened in their parish lives. And I think they appreciated my concern for young people and what was happening in their lives, particularly those that I was confirming and receiving into the church. And I think people saw me as genuine.*

Douglas: *Is there any advice you would give to those black women, in particular, who might follow you in becoming bishop?*

Harris: *Never get too big for your britches. No. No, no, no. Being elected bishop doesn't make you the greatest person in the world.*

"A Good Ride"

Harris: *Um, well one question you did ask me and I guess I left out a piece of it, you asked me what I was proud of, and that is that people still call on me to be with them in ministry in retirement. In preaching and other aspects of ministry in retirement.*

Douglas: *What do you miss about being an active bishop?*

Harris: *I miss being involved on a regular basis with the people of the diocese. And I am humbly proud that something the magnitude of the Barbara C. Harris Camp and Conference Center came into being and that it serves not only a large number of young people in the diocese but is a conference facility or meeting facility for other groups in and out of the church. And I always referred to it as Tom Shaw's insurance company because I said there's a great danger in naming something of that magnitude for somebody while they're still living, and so he has ensured that I will try to behave myself for the rest of my life.*

Douglas: *What do you hope your legacy to be, Barbara?*

Harris: *I would hope faithful service to the best of your limited ability, because we all have limitations. Nobody has it all.*

All in all, it's been quite a ride though this life. I wonder what my great-grandmother, raised as a slave, would think about where we are now. I think about all the struggles of my people, personified for me in my family and in our hurts, the barriers that were set before us, and in the victories that we've won, which weren't just for ourselves. What I do know is that even though things have changed, we aren't far enough along, not by a long shot. Black people have to keep on keeping on and to be less patient, not more. People have criticized me for speaking out, for being feisty (which as far as I'm concerned, is just another word for "uppity"), but I'd criticize myself for not being feisty (or uppity, take your choice) enough. I think we people of color and women shouldn't worry so much about blending in, but stand out for who we are and be proud of carrying our flag into the battle.

With the help of so many people, we've done a lot, and now the time has come for me to get some rest (not that anyone really believes I'll do that). As I look back over all that's happened, the victories and defeats, the moving ahead two steps and back down one, I'm satisfied that with the grace of God we've persevered and been as faithful as we could, which is all that God has asked us to be.

Douglas: *Listening to your story, really it's amazing, first of all, the humility and most of all the fact that you're a remarkable woman.*

Harris: *I never thought of that, of myself as remarkable.*

Douglas: *How do you think of yourself, how do you see your whole journey now?*

Harris: *I think I did a good job. I think I really did do a good job. I'm not saying outstanding, but a good job. And I think I fulfilled my responsibilities well and I know that God has been faithful and graceful to me so I can say to God and to you, Hallelujah anyhow!*

AFTERWORD

Barbara, Hallelujah!

I met Bishop Harris in the spring of 1977. My rector had invited me to a meeting at a Roman Catholic retreat center in Los Angeles. The board of the *Witness* magazine, which was just being reactivated, was hosting gatherings around the church. I walked into the room and immediately my eyes focused on the small, attractive African American woman with a large Afro hair style who had a cigarette in her hand. She looked like me, only six or seven inches shorter; my hair was also way out there. As the only two African Americans in the room, we bonded immediately, beyond hair and color.

Two years later, Barbara returned to Los Angeles and preached at St. John's Episcopal Church, my home parish. By this time, she was a transitional deacon. As I was just discerning my call to ordination, I asked her how she was able to get ordained and still work. She told me her story, how she studied part time in Philadelphia and even went to England for classes. She said it was not easy but she did what she had to do and she encouraged me to find a way as well. At that time, I had two children in college and worked full time.

Every ten years the archbishop of Canterbury hosts all the bishops of the Anglican Communion to meet to discuss the mission of the church in a variety of areas. At the Lambeth Conference in 1988 I was invited to be the first ordained woman to address the bishops. Barbara was not only a source of support but also a friend in need. There was a photo of me, Barbara, and Sarah Motley. The caption questioned if we were planning some protest. In reality, I was asking Barbara to pick up an electrical convertor for my curling iron.

At the time women were not allowed to be ordained in many of the places in the Anglican Communion. There was much controversy about my upcoming speech. Before my address to the bishops, Barbara advised me to speak up and not be afraid, as my speech was excellent. They were words and support I definitely needed.

When Barbara was nominated for suffragan bishop of Massachusetts, the nomination and subsequent election caused much conflict in the church. Yet she continued to model for all of us how to live with grace under intense pressure. Even at her consecration, there were formal protests. After the protests were heard, the presiding bishop said the service would continue. The eight thousand present loudly applauded and shouted "Hallelujah!"

As bishop, Barbara continued to speak out in support of women, lay and ordained, as many did not support the ordination of women. When I went to the Diocese of Atlanta in 1989, two clergy left to become Roman Catholic priests because of the ordination of women and Barbara's election. One time, when I met with the vestry of a congregation in the diocese, the senior warden called the bishop's office and told them they did not want a woman or a priest of color to be assigned to them. Barbara was very helpful to me as I navigated instances of gender and racial bias. She had experienced it before me.

The ramifications of Barbara's witness and ministry in the church were manifested in several events. The election and consecration of the Right Reverend Jennifer Baskerville-Burroughs, the first African American woman diocesan bishop, is a direct result of the ministry of Barbara Harris, as are all the women bishops who have followed her. The election of the Right Reverend Katharine Jefferts Schori, the first woman to be our presiding bishop, and the election of the Right Reverend Michael Curry, the first African American presiding bishop, are both results of the ministry of Barbara Harris.

In 2017, the Episcopal Women's History Project hosted the first ever conference of women of color. Over fifty women of color from around the country met for the first time and shared their stories of pain, of struggle, of hope in the church. They were all able to tell their stories, especially the young women, because Barbara Harris had gone before them and told her story. For that they said "Hallelujah."

But as Bishop Harris continues to say, *a luta continua*. The struggle continues. The struggle continues.

Nan A. Peete

TRYING TO
PREACH THE WORD

Consecration of DeDe Duncan-Probe Diocese of Central New York December 3, 2016

May only truth be spoken here and may only truth be heard. In the name of Christ, Amen. Good morning, church.

It is an honor to serve as the homilist this morning, my second time for a woman diocesan. And since we have much ahead of us today, I will try to be mercifully brief.

I think it is significant that the new episcopate we inaugurate here today takes place early in the start of a new Christian church year. Tomorrow marks the Second Sunday of Advent. Recently, I saw a line in an issue of a popular religious journal which read, "Advent signals the possibility and hope of a fresh start." And that is exactly what is taking place here today—a fresh and, yes, a different start in an age-old tradition—for this diocese and for the church in this corner of the vineyard.

The words of the prophet Isaiah ring loud and true as we heard in our first reading; "The spirit of the Lord God" indeed has been "bestowed" upon our sister and her charge is clear: to lead the people of this diocese—clergy and lay—in bringing "good news to the poor; to bind up the broken hearted, to proclaim liberty to captives and release to those in the prison of desperation and despair." The rest of the charge rings with equal clarity and I need not cite it in its familiar entirety.

To live into that charge demands a holy boldness that my own bishop recently exhorted the people of the Diocese of Massachusetts to embrace and live into. "Strategizing to recreate the church of the past," he warned, "will not reveal to us how to be the church of Jesus Christ today and tomorrow."

He further urged (and again, I quote) a "metanoia—a change of mind that allows for letting go of past perceptions and of fear. We must celebrate and give thanks for the blessings of our history to be sure," he continued, "and we must listen for new ways in which God is calling us to respond to the world, even now."

I would suggest that this is true for the whole church—not just here at home, but across the globe.

Thus, I would suggest that as we gather to consecrate a new bishop this morning, we all need to recommit to being willing, active, unabashed members of what our presiding bishop and primate, since his election and seating, has reminded us is "the Jesus Movement." And he has shared with us clearly what that commitment entails.

Having quoted our scripture, my bishop, and our PB, I now have some personal words for our bishop-elect, to which I invite you all to listen in. I have shared some of these thoughts with at least two other women as they moved into their episcopates, and I hope I will have an opportunity to share them with others in months and years ahead.

My sister DeDe: Soon the bishops here present, acting for the community of faith, will set their seal upon you. You will be charged, ordained, and entrusted with a new and wider ministry to which you bring your unique gifts and a demonstrated love for God's people. You have enjoyed a rich lay and ordained ministry in the dioceses of New York, Massachusetts, and Virginia. But not all that you have done in the past specifically prepares you for some of the challenges you will face in the days ahead. Through it all, remember *who* you are, *whose* you are, and that you come among God's people to serve them by enabling their ministries.

During your examination you will be asked, among other things, if you will boldly proclaim and interpret the gospel of Christ, enlightening the minds and stirring up the conscience of your people. And your response must be "I will in the power of the Spirit." Your best efforts in this regard will not always be understood, appreciated, or welcomed. In both word and deed, you must proclaim redemption, liberation, hope, and love. And you must also proclaim judgement, reminding folk that we cannot go back to the Garden of Eden, but instead must step into the new age, not knowing what its final shape will be. But as we are reminded by that old gospel hymn: "We have come this far by faith, leaning on the Lord," and we trust our God for the next step of the journey.

You must not demur from urging folk out of the comfortable pew and challenging them to seek the welfare of the city and the suburbs alike, for the problems of the city eventually become the problems of those suburban communities. On some days you will see your role with great clarity and you may be tempted to paraphrase Professor Henry Higgins in the musical *My Fair Lady* and say: "I've got it; I've got it, by Jove, I think I've got it." And on others, probably more numerous, I suspect you will feel like you are trying to put pantyhose on an octopus.

Stand up my sister, if you will:

Shortly, in addition to the Holy Scriptures, from which you will be charged to feed and tend the flock of Christ, you will be presented with some symbols of your office as bishop. Remember, they are only symbols. They point to a deeper reality of life, but they are *not* the reality of life. You will receive a ring, a symbol of authority—but it is only a ring; it is not your life. Your authority demands integrity, accountability, and service. You will receive a staff, a sign of the shepherd's office. The shepherd's responsibility entails endless care of the flock entrusted to the shepherd's charge. But remember, it is a staff only—a symbol. It is not your life. A miter will be placed on your head as a crown of fire, evocative of the flames of the Spirit which fell, unbidden, upon the disciples on the day of Pentecost. It, too, is symbolic; it is only a miter. It is not your life.

Now, remember this: It is prayer that is your life and prayer that is your lifeline. My mentor, the late John Thomas Walker, bishop of Washington, DC, exhorted: "Pray often, sing when you can, weep daily over the city, and wash the feet of the weak and the lowly, the black and the white, the poor and the rich, the sick and the healthy, the believer and the unbeliever."

God bless you, my sister, and may you go from strength to strength in Christ's joyful service, knowing and never forgetting the truth of these words, spoken to me by a dynamic Pentecostal woman preacher as I entered episcopal orders: "The power behind you is greater than the task ahead of you." Amen.

Easter III (Acts 9:1–20)

Reflecting on our first lesson for this morning, I am reminded of the old adage: "There are none so blind as those who will not see."

History is filled with examples of humankind's stubborn dogged pursuit of wild schemes and dreams with a single-minded determination that can only be called obsession. Individuals and groups have persistently and relentlessly pressed themselves toward some end with the force of a bulldozer smashing everything in its path. Rulers and their armies, religious zealots, governments and groups committed to various causes comprise an almost endless list. In each instance, some force greater than they had to be placed in their path to stop them in their tracks and bring them to a grinding halt. It is the nature of humankind in every age to be on a collision course with history.

Such is the situation we find in our lesson from the Acts of the Apostles, where Luke recounts the dramatic conversion of Saul of Tarsus on the road to Damascus. It is a story that excites the imagination and as a youngster I used to think that Saul deserved what he got and more besides.

Saul: well educated, devout, highly intelligent, but an ambassador of hate. He was headed from Jerusalem to Damascus with one purpose—to arrest the followers of Jesus—called followers of the "Way"—and bring them back to Jerusalem in chains.

He was well known for his zeal in this regard in Jerusalem and he carried with him credentials from the high priests. But Saul was stopped in his tracks. Blinded by a light from heaven, as if struck by lightning, he was knocked down by God. Sometimes God has to knock us on our backsides to get our attention.

More important than what happened to Saul physically out there on the Damascus road is, of course, the result of his encounter with God. It was a dramatic event, yes, but more than an event. It was an experience. We can live through events largely unaffected, but experiences change us. This experience changed Saul from fierce enemy of the Christian faith to Paul, its foremost apostle. It changed him from persecutor to promoter.

Saul had his plan but it got turned around completely by God's plan. Saul's plan was to clean house and to get rid of those he thought were tampering with orthodox religion. But God had an eternal plan which predated Saul's and was destined to outlast and outlive it.

What really happened out there on the Damascus road? Paul lost his physical sight to point out that he had lost his spiritual sight. His spiritual sight was impaired because he was trying to deny what he knew was right. In reality, Paul already was a Christian in his heart of hearts. God knew that! God said to Ananias—"Go to him, he is my chosen vessel." Go to him, he is my instrument.

Paul had already been a Christian a long time, only unconsciously. That is why he had such a fanatical resistance to Christians. Fanaticism usually is found in individuals who are trying to compensate for their secret doubts. The incident on the way to Damascus marks the moment when what was unconscious in Paul broke through into his consciousness. He had been unable to conceive of himself as a Christian because he was resisting Christ. He became physically blind and could regain his sight only when he submitted himself fully to Christ.

Paul had a psychological blindness or what is called psychogenetic blindness because of his unwillingness to see and to understand or to realize that something in his life, something in his subconscious, was incompatible with his conscious attitude and his conscious behavior. He not only had to be stopped, he had to be reversed, converted. And by his conversion he was made over and remolded into something new.

Our global society needs a Damascus road experience. This world, this country, our communities, our church, all need a conversion. We, too, need personal conversion. The time for such a conversion has long been upon us.

If there is not a religious experience soon that changes the way people see themselves in relationship to other people as nations, as races, as political ideologists, as individuals, we are headed for certain destruction because we not only are on a collision course with history, we are on a collision course with God. Something must change! Our religious experience may not come as a blinding light from heaven, but we need a dramatic conversion and we need it right now. From the highest levels of government to individuals, the prevailing attitude is "my way or no way."

We are blinded to that reality because it is easier to focus on other people's faults. We don't see the inconsistencies and the incompatibilities within ourselves because we don't want to see them. We have difficulty acknowledging that someone else might be right because we don't want to acknowledge that we might be wrong. We need a conversion!

Saul sits in high places today. Around the world Saul sits in the halls of government and condemns all who do not acknowledge the superiority of its way of life and threatens to unleash its military might on them. But, the psalmist tells us, "a king does not win because of its powerful army; a soldier does not triumph because of his strength" (Ps. 33:16).

Saul walks the streets of the cities and seeks to undermine those who do not share his belief that "I've got mine and you must get yours the best way you can" or "take care of number one first, and after that anything goes." We need a conversion!

Saul's blindness allows us to benefit from the exploited labor of migrant and undocumented workers with little or no thought about the conditions under which they work and live.

Saul's blindness is in the church. It resists change under the seven-word rubric "we have always done it this way." It wants to lay exclusive claim on God's revelation of truth and to condemn others who search for new interpretations of that truth. We need a conversion!

We need a conversion experience no matter what heights we have achieved, how important we think we are, what accolades we receive or how much we think we know about God.

Paul—"Hebrew among Hebrews"—had to confess, as should we, "I do not the good I want, but the evil I do not want is what I do. Now if I do what I do not want, it is no longer I that do it but sin which dwells in me."

We can move from such remorse to resolution. We can remove the conflict within us. We can be rid of the inconsistency of what we say and what we do. We can do away with the incompatibility of our lifestyle with our baptismal covenant.

The scales can fall from our eyes if we are willing to see the way of Christ and to hear his voice as he calls us to stop persecuting him by oppressing others. We need to call on the name of the Lord and pray: convert your world, O Lord, beginning with me. Amen.

Walking Stations of the Cross—Washington, DC 2016
Second Station

Jesus Takes up His Cross at the Martin Luther King, Jr. Memorial

As the meditation commentary and the prayers for this station clearly indicate, Jesus willingly endured the shame and agony associated with bearing the cross on the long walk to Calvary and his execution there for the redemption of all humanity. He might have sought an easier path, but we must ask if a more comfortable, less sacrificial role would have accomplished our redemption and our salvation.

Similarly, Dr. Martin Luther King Jr., memorialized here, might have chosen to carry out a singly focused, more comfortable ministry of leading a thriving congregation; while such a ministry would not have been without some difficulties—to which many of us could attest—it was not predestined to lead to hardship, self-sacrifice, danger, arrest and jail, and ultimately death by execution on his own Calvary, the balcony of the Lorraine Hotel in Memphis, Tennessee.

In the tradition of Jesus, Dr. King willingly took up a cross to lead a movement that affirmed the value and dignity of every human life despite the color of skin in which it is encased.

Jesus, said, "The first commandment is this: love the Lord your God with all your heart, with all your soul, with all your mind, and with all your strength. The second is this: love your neighbor as yourself. There is no other commandment greater than these."

Brother Martin fleshed out the modern embodiment of these commandments in his memorable speech "I Have a Dream," delivered not very far from where this pilgrimage is now paused.

The question for us is are we willing to shoulder up the cross for justice and bear it as did Jesus and, in the tradition of Jesus, as did Martin, to the mount of sacrifice that also became the mount of salvation.

As this pilgrimage continues, this would be my prayer:

Holy God give strength to our spiritual arms to willingly take up the crosses yet to be carried and to bear them to the Calvary of this life and for the Calvary of those yet to come. Amen.

Historic St. Thomas—Women's Day

In the name of God: Creator, Liberator and Sustainer. Amen.

Good morning, church. What a joy to be with you on this special Sunday and I am honored by your kind invitation to join in this annual observance of Women's Day.

I want to call your attention to a familiar story from scripture found in the fourth chapter of the Gospel according to John. We find there an interesting encounter that begins with a little verbal sparring match between our Lord and a woman who has come to draw water from the well of Jacob. As we try to put this encounter into some focus and some context, I ask you to think with me on the subject, "A Thirst for the Kingdom."

As I reflected on this passage of scripture with its detailed encounter between Jesus and the Samaritan woman, I was mindful of the fact that we usually hold up as examples women of unquestioned character, unblemished reputation, and solid achievement, especially on a day such as this when we celebrate women of legacy, faith and hope. And certainly many quickly come to mind, not only from the pages of scripture, but from everyday life as well. We tend to focus on the virtues of womanhood and, again, almost everyone here could extol these. Moreover, we tend to highlight strengths rather than weaknesses, fine points rather than faults, and sterling qualities rather than sins. We usually hold up the "perfect," but in this text we learn something from the "imperfect."

Jesus, on his way from Judea to Galilee, is passing through Samaria. He is passing through unfriendly territory. The rivalry between Jews and Samaritans was well known; it had existed from the time of Ezra and Nehemiah. Jews and Samaritans had serious theological differences. Jews didn't think much of Samaritans, for Samaritans had profaned the sacred altars of the Jews by letting pigs run loose through the temple. In fact, to the Jews, Samaritans were not only unclean, they were barbaric. That is why the disciples and others were shocked when Jesus used the parable of the Good Samaritan to illustrate his answer to the question: "Who is my neighbor?"

They also were caught up short by the story of the cleansing of the ten lepers; the only one who returned to give thanks was a Samaritan. The Jews could not believe that Jesus would use a Samaritan as a good example of anything.

So it is odd that, although weary from his journey and the midday heat, our Lord would stop to rest in this hostile place. Most of us would try to get through hostile territory and on to familiar or neutral, if not safe ground as quickly as possible. But Jesus, as on so many occasions in his life and ministry, chooses an odd place to stop and to witness to the glory and the love of God. And he stops in the odd places of our lives.

It was not unusual, however, that Jesus—who often broke with tradition—would request water, even from a stranger, even from a member of an enemy group, even from a woman. Water was life-sustaining in that parched and barren land. His disciples, we are told, had gone off to buy food. But even though one could survive without food, one could not go for long without water. And his request was one that would not be denied, even from a sworn enemy. Life was much more simple in that time; there were just certain things you did not deny people. Scripture was very clear on hospitality to strangers. So Jesus says to this woman with her water jar, "Give me a drink."

But our Lord is after more than just water. Jesus, resting at this fork in the road between Judea and Galilee, in the course of his journey to his ultimate earthly destination—Jerusalem and Calvary—also is at a spiritual crossroads. His mission is coming full cycle as he makes his tortuous journey that culminates in our salvation. And he is about to do something he has not done before. Here he reveals to this woman of the hated Samaritans, this woman of questionable repute, something he has refrained from revealing to others who might be regarded as more worthy of his attention. Jesus reveals to this woman in no uncertain terms that he is the Messiah.

There have been other occasions up to this point on which the Father's glory has been shown through the Son and on which he carefully had told others that it was not yet time to lay out the full story. At the wedding feast at Cana of Galilee where he turned water into wine, he told his mother his hour had not yet come. And like a mother who knows there is something special about her child she said—"all right, son" and she told the wedding hosts "just do whatever he tells you."

Again, on the Mount of Transfiguration, where he was caught up between Moses and Elijah and shone forth in radiant dazzling beauty, he cautioned his disciples to tell no one of what they had been privileged to see. He gave similar warnings in some of his miracles of healing. Yet here at this crossroads, he makes himself known to this woman.

As if to further document his revelation, he goes on to tell this woman about herself. He blows her cover as if to reinforce the truth that before God, the secrets of all hearts shall be revealed.

It shocks us when somebody sees through us and discovers what we would rather keep hidden. We go to great lengths to try to cover up our secrets and our faults. We make sure we are seen with the right people in the right places at the right time; we join the proper organizations and institutions, including the church. Well, we may be able to fool our friends and neighbors, but we can't fool Jesus!

It is human nature to try to cover up the unflattering, the unattractive, the uncomfortable things about our lives. At first the woman at the well tries to be cagey. She tries to dodge the question and the issue. "Go and get your husband," Jesus instructs her. "Sir," she says, "I have no husband." "Right on," says Jesus, and proceeds to detail her liaisons and her indiscretions. "You've had five husbands and the man you have now is not your husband." Imagine our reaction if personally confronted that way by Jesus today; as our elders might have said, "Now look here Jesus, you done left off preaching and gone to meddling!" She also challenges him when he says, "if you knew who you were talking to and what God is offering you, you would be the one asking 'give me a drink.' And He would give you living water." "Are you greater than our father Jacob who gave us this well?" she asks. But Jesus stays right on the case. "Everyone who drinks of this water will thirst again, but whosoever drinks of the water I shall give will never thirst."

Ultimately this woman realizes that she is conversing with someone different, someone special, somebody with something to offer, someone who could make a difference in her life. And that's what Jesus is all about—making a difference in our lives, helping us to emerge into our full stature as children of God, not only women, but *people* of legacy, faith and hope.

I think there are some clear messages for us in this strange story of the woman at the well: messages for us as we stand at our individual and personal crossroads and ponder the choices of life in a vain world that is no friend to grace; messages as we consider ourselves as emerging people of Christ's kingdom; messages for us as we realize, as did the woman at the well, that while we are not yet what we should be, thank God, we are not what we were. We are different because God has touched our lives, different because we realize we can learn from all of God's people, even from folk like the Samaritan woman—a street woman if you will.

No matter what you think of the Samaritan woman, a fact— and an important fact—is that *she was at the well*. She was there where Jesus was. Had she not gone to the well when she did, she would not have been privileged to meet and have an encounter with the Savior.

No matter her reason for going at the odd hour she went (and scholars tell us she didn't go at the usual time, at the early dawn or in the cool of the evening). She went in the burning heat of the day when the sun was scorching, when everybody else was looking for some shade or for some relief from the midday heat. No matter her reason for going at that hour, she was at the right place at the right time. If you don't go near the well, you cannot draw up water. You must make yourself present and available to receive the living water God so freely gives. You must go to the well!

Too many people are absent from the well. Because the woman came, she received a blessing. Simply because she came she received a blessing. So many stay away and or do not avail themselves of the blessings that can be theirs.

People stay away for various reasons. Some feel like the Samaritan woman—scorned and derided because they lead different kinds of lives. Others feel rejected because of who and what they are. Some stay away because they don't want to rub shoulders with those they consider undesirable, those who don't fit in for one reason or another, those who are poor or shabby.

Some get so locked up in their own troubles, their own trials and tribulations, so trapped in that small box of self-pity, they are absent from the well. Some are so caught up in the pastimes and pleasures of this world, they absent themselves from the well. Singing as we hear in that hymn almost persuaded "Go Spirit, go Thy way, some more convenient day, on Thee I'll call." Some are so puffed up with self-righteousness, they don't even think they need a drink.

People are absent from the well not realizing Jesus can give them a new heart, a new mind, a new song to sing, a new way of looking at life, a new way of loving other people—even the unlovable—if they have a thirst for the kingdom.

Another fact to remember is that the Samaritan woman brought a vessel. If you are young or never lived in the country or visited a rural area or foreign nation where folks rely on wells, you may not know about drawing water. Getting water from a well is not like cupping your hands or holding a glass under a faucet or pressing a button on a water fountain. If you are going to make use of a well, you must bring something with which to draw water. The woman told Jesus, "Sir you have nothing to draw with and the well is deep."

That is true of God's grace. Too many of us come to the well empty-handed. We bring no vessel in which to draw up the living water.

People say, "I come to church, but I don't get anything out of it." If you don't bring anything in which or with which to get something, then you won't get anything. We bring to the throne of grace the thin shells of ourselves instead of open, trusting hearts and souls, vessels in which to draw up the living water. If you don't believe God can do something for you, you'll never know when or what God does.

Lastly, the Samaritan woman not only received a blessing, she went and told others. "Come see a man who told me all that I ever did." Come see for yourself. The woman at the well became a well woman and shared her wholeness with others.

Too many of us do not share what has been given to us. If we would witness to what we have received, others might be moved to come and receive also. When is the last time you told somebody what the Lord has done for you? When is the last time you shared with someone that he's brought you "a mighty long way?"

My friends, we thirst after many things in this world. We thirst after money, power, prestige, position. We put our trust in them, we even pray about them. But like our Lord, we too are at a crossroads, in the church and in society. We still have a choice and the question our Lord is asking us is do we have a thirst for the kingdom?

Jesus is asking us: Are you content to settle for the temporary thirst quenchers of life; the material values of this world, the right connections, the proper credentials, the things on which this society places so much value, things that will never slake the thirst of our parched dry souls? Or do you thirst after righteousness, thirst after peace, thirst after justice, thirst after the liberation of all of God's people?

Do we thirst after those things that make for a just society as Jesus proclaimed the kingdom to be? If we gave our testimony this morning would we sing with the psalmist, "Like the hart desireth the water brooks, so longeth my soul after thee, O Lord," or sing with the elders, "I heard the voice of Jesus say, 'Behold I freely give. The living waters, thirsty one, stoop down and drink and live.' I came to Jesus and I drank of that life-giving stream. My thirst was quenched, my soul revived and now I live in him." Do we have a thirst for the living water with which God truly enriches our lives? Do we have a thirst to emerge as faithful Christians to be more than we are? Do we have a thirst for the kingdom? Each of us must respond for herself or himself. Jesus is patiently waiting for our answer. Amen.

Eulogy

Van Samuel Bird—Pastor, Priest, Mentor and Friend

For those of us who were privileged to walk a part of our Christian journey in the company of Van Bird, we found in him an encouraging, supportive, loving truth-teller, who held up to the light of day his own and our flaws and weaknesses and by examining them, helped us better mold and develop our God-given strengths and gifts.

A prayer Van frequently offered before preaching was this simple petition:

> O God, the light of the minds which know you, the joy of the hearts which love you, the strength of the wills which try to serve you: Grant us to know you, so as to love you, to love you so as to serve you, in whose service is perfect freedom. And since you have called all of us to your service, make us worthy of that calling and empower us for that service, through Jesus Christ our Lord.

And that prayer was the hallmark of his life.

As my principal mentor throughout my somewhat unusual and unorthodox preparation for ordained ministry and especially for my "ten rounds" with the Commission on Ministry and its academic sub-committee, Van took me to the ecclesiastical /theological "gym" more than once—sparring to test not only my academic strength, but my spiritual stamina and reflexes as well.

Van Bird's ministry in this church was not easy. It was at times disappointing and discouraging, but he remained steadfast in God's call and persevered to the end.

If there is some one thing I think we can learn from the life of this brother and friend, it is this: Van showed us through his life and ministry that we are prisoners of hope. But more than simply prisoners of hope, he showed us that we are Easter people. He showed us that we are an Easter people, moving through a Good Friday world.

One of the sterling qualities and characteristics of Easter people is faithfulness. They hang on until the end, like the women who stood and stayed at the foot of the cross.

The great orator and abolitionist, Frederick Douglas, once said: "You don't get everything you pay for in life, but you pay for everything you get." While it is difficult to dispute the basic truth of that statement, the one thing we do not pay for is grace—what our elders called "free grace," undying love.

It was grace that allowed Job through all his travail and woe to proclaim: "I know that my redeemer lives and my eyes shall behold him and not a stranger." It was grace that put a song in the heart of Mary, the God-bearer, and caused her to say: "My soul magnifies the Lord and my spirit rejoices in God, my savior."

It was grace that moved John Newton, captain of a slave ship, to weary of trafficking in human flesh and, after years of trying, to become a priest of the church and to give us, among many others, that hymn to which we so often turn for comfort: "Amazing grace, how sweet the sound."

The prophet Jeremiah asked: "Is there no balm in Gilead, is there no physician there?" And it was grace that enabled our slave forbearers, though chained and shackled, to sing: "There is a balm in Gilead to make the wounded whole."

It was grace that enabled Van to live a life that exemplified the belief that we've come this far by faith and we trust our God for the next step of the journey and the determination that I will go, I shall go to see what the end will be.

It is grace that will enable you, Eva, and this family and host of friends to give over a cherished husband, father, grandfather, brother and friend to a gracious and loving God who has opened to him the gates of larger life and who, we trust, will receive him more and more into His joyful service.

Thanks be to God for giving us Van as a companion in the way.

Absalom Jones Service

Let there be peace among us and let us not be instruments of our own or others' oppression. In the name of God: Creator, Liberator and Sustainer. Amen.

Good afternoon, church! It is a joy (and an honor) to be with you as we commemorate and celebrate the life and witness of Absalom Jones, the first black priest in the Episcopal Church and unofficial bishop of its small early knot of black communicants, as well as shepherd to many other sheep that were not of this fold. Fortuitously and significantly, the church's observance comes in the midst of Black History Month on the secular calendar.

First off, let me ask the ordained ministers of the church present to raise your hand if you spent more than one or two years as a transitional deacon before being advanced to the priesthood. Absalom was ordained a deacon in 1795 and spent nine years in that order before being ordained priest in 1804.

One of the striking things to me about Absalom Jones is how faithfully he, and his friend Richard Allen—founder and first bishop of the African Methodist Episcopal or AME Church—and the people they both led lived into the words of the prophet Isaiah, contained in the first lesson appointed for this observance. Words uttered again by Jesus as he began his ministry in the synagogue at Nazareth when he threw down the gauntlet to the powers that be in Israel and delineated the scope and parameters of the exercise of that ministry.

"The spirit of the Lord God is upon me, because the Lord has anointed me, he has sent me to bring good news to the oppressed, to bind up the broken hearted, to proclaim liberty to the captives and release to the prisoners to proclaim the year of the Lord's favor. . . ." (And then Jesus had the chutzpah or audacity to add, "Today this scripture has been fulfilled in your hearing.")

Jones and Allen did indeed attempt to do those things under the most difficult of circumstances and their success perhaps surprised themselves most of all as they exercised their ministry. And, much as we find today, it was fellow Christians—then the leadership of the Methodist Church in Philadelphia—that tried to thwart their efforts.

We learn a little something of Absalom Jones' life and ministry from his page in *Lesser Feasts and Fasts*, now known as *Holy Women, Holy Men*. We know, for instance, that he was born a slave in 1746 in Delaware; that he taught himself to read from the New Testament, among other books; when he was sixteen he was sold to a store owner in Philadelphia; that he attended a night school for blacks, operated by Quakers; that at twenty he married another slave and unselfishly purchased her freedom with his earnings before purchasing his own.

We also learn that he served as a lay minister for the black membership of St. George's Methodist Episcopal Church. The active evangelism of Jones and Richard Allen greatly increased black membership at St. George's, where they contributed from their meager finances and gave of their substantial labor—laying floors and building the gallery, to which the alarmed vestry intended they be relegated during worship, without notifying them beforehand. And we have the oft-repeated story that when ushers roughly tried to forcibly remove them during prayer, Absalom and his fellow blacks walked out en mass never to return and, if you will pardon the expression, darken their doors again.

But it is a manuscript by Richard Allen—written several years after the establishment of St. Thomas Church—that tells the real hardscrabble story of the founding of the Free African Society and their efforts to establish a house of worship by and for free or emancipated black people in Philadelphia. And it is important to note that it was by and for free blacks, because they felt, thereby, they could help emancipate other blacks still held in bondage.

The manuscript, dictated by Allen who could neither read nor write, and written for him by his son, tells in minute detail the circumstances which finally led to "the parting of the ways" with the Methodists and the eventual development of the Free African Society—a mutual benefit or aid association—into an Episcopal church. I found it in a precious volume, long out of print, published in 1922 that was given to my grandmother by our parish rector at Christmas 1928 and passed on to me by my mother at Easter 1974.

It is titled *The History of the Afro-American Group of the Episcopal Church* and was written by the Reverend Dr. George Freeman Bragg Jr., longtime rector of St. James African Episcopal Church in Baltimore, whom I am old enough to remember and who had two sons follow him into ordained ministry. I believe the book has recently been reprinted.

As the fledgling church was getting underway there was a discussion about the denomination with which it would affiliate. Interestingly, only Jones and Allen wanted to remain Methodist. They were outvoted by those who wanted to affiliate with the establishment connected Episcopal Church. According to the Allen manuscript, his and Jones' reasoning was as follows:

Notwithstanding we have been so violently persecuted by the elders, we are in favor of being attached to the Methodist connection, for I was confident there was no religious sect or denomination that would suit the capacity of colored people as well as the Methodists, for the plain and simple gospel suits best for any people, for the unlearned can understand and learned are sure to understand; and the reason that the Methodists are so successful in the awakening and conversion of the colored people is the plain doctrine and having a good discipline.

I mention that only to say that there is a piece of the Methodist discipline that could serve the Episcopal Church very well today. Every member of the Methodist Society belonged and perhaps still does to a class as in school class. Each class had a class leader, a layman or lay elder, who held class meetings and who went in search of or to check up on class members who absented themselves from worship. They then knew if someone was ill, or in trouble, or just derelict in their Christian duty. Not a bad idea, if you ask me. Such an effort on the part of lay people might stem some of the current tide of our declining numbers.

I have another question for the lay and ordained ministers—anyone here know someone whose given name is Absalom? I have never personally known anyone with that odd name. The only other Absalom of whom I have known was Absalom, the son of David.

A few years ago, a young priest in Massachusetts drew several vivid contrasts between the character and deeds of Absalom Jones and those of Absalom, the son of David. I will not try to recount all of them for you, I could not begin to do justice to his commentary, rather simply say the latter was what some of us today would call a prismatic son of a female dog—and we all know the shorthand for that. By that I mean to simply say that looking at Absalom, son of David, through a prism, he would be the same thing from any angle you view him. Our young priest's contrasts of the two Absaloms drove me back to the Second Book of Samuel to reread the exploits of this arrogant, selfish, self-serving young man who plotted and schemed in almost unimaginable ways to dispose of his father and usurp the throne. Among other things, he dishonored his father's concubines in plain sight, which given the number, was a feat in and of itself. The account of young prince Absalom's scheming and plotting reads like a John Grisham crime novel. I say that with authority, since I am a Grisham junkie. By contrast, Absalom Jones, a slave but with honorable intentions, was a prince in the true sense of the title.

Back to Absalom and his ministry. One aspect of that ministry that is not included in *Lesser Feasts and Fasts* or in the Allen
manuscript is this: The late 1790s saw the city of Philadelphia
gripped by an epidemic of yellow fever.

Jones, Richard Allen, and members of the Free African
Society went about the city tending white people who had been
stricken by the fever and burying those who had died, neither
of whom other whites would touch. Despite their healing mission, Jones and his people had to enter white homes through
the back door like tradesmen and servants. But minister they
did. And servants they were—servants of the most high God.
Sometimes we have to go through the back door to do and
to be what God is calling us to be and to do. Sometimes we
must, as my grandmother would say, "take low" to accomplish
the right thing, as Absalom did in purchasing his wife's freedom, before securing his own. After all, we are not striding in
a Macy's Thanksgiving Day parade or strutting our stuff in a
Tournament of Roses spectacular. Rather we are called to walk
humbly with that thin line of the faithful who honor Micah's
verbs to do justice and to love mercy. As the late educator and
biblical scholar Verna Dozier often reminded us, we need to
stop reversing Micah's verbs, whereby we love justice and do
some mercy.

Absalom Jones was known as an earnest preacher. He
denounced slavery and warned oppressors to "clean their
hands of slaves." It is said that to him God was the Father
who always acted "on behalf of the oppressed and distressed."
But it was his constant visiting and mild manner that made
him beloved by his own flock and by the community. Known
as "the Black Bishop of the Episcopal Church," it also is said
that Jones was an example of persistent faith in God and
in the church as God's instrument. Can I get an amen for
Absalom Jones and for Richard Allen and for the people who
helped to establish historic St. Thomas African Episcopal
Church (which, to this day—under the rectorship of a man

with most delightful and delicious name, the Rev. Martini Shaw—carries on ministry begun some 225 years ago)? And while we're at it, can I get an amen for the faithful witness of all those, lay and ordained, who minister in the spirit of blessed Absalom? Amen.

Final Shout

When you're feeling down and out,
Throw your hands up high and shout Hallelujah anyhow.
'cause I'm wrapped up, tied up,
tangled up in Jesus.
Singing Hallelujah anyhow.

A TRIBUTE TO THE RT. REV BARBARA C. HARRIS ON THE 25TH ANNIVERSARY OF HER CONSECRATION AS BISHOP

Whereas, Barbara C. Harris was born in the Diocese of Pennsylvania on June 12, 1930 and received her early Christian formation at St. Barnabas Episcopal Church in Philadelphia, and

Whereas, throughout her ministry as a lay leader, deacon, priest, and bishop of the church she has been a champion for racial justice and the rights of women and gay, lesbian, and transgendered persons, an advocate for the poor, and an activist in environmental and anti-nuclear concerns, and

Whereas, she was elected bishop suffragan of the Diocese of Massachusetts on September 24, 1988, and was consecrated February 11, 1989 at Hynes Auditorium in Boston before a congregation of eight thousand persons, thus making her the first woman bishop of the Episcopal Church and in the Anglican Communion, and

Whereas, she served admirably and faithfully in that ministry until she retired in 2003, exercising her special prophetic gifts as an African American woman "to guard the faith, unity and discipline of the church; to ordain priests and deacons and to join in ordaining bishops; and to be in all things a faithful pastor and wholesome example for the entire flock of Christ and to share in the leadership of the church throughout the world," and served as co-chair of the House of Bishops Committee on Racism, which composed the *House of Bishops Pastoral Letter on the Sin of Racism*, and

Whereas, she "stood in the breach so others could pass over," thus paving the way for 19 more women to be consecrated bishops in the Episcopal Church and fifteen others to be consecrated across the worldwide Anglican Communion and

Whereas, upon her retirement, the Diocese of Massachusetts established in her honor the Barbara C. Harris Camp and Conference Center, and

Whereas, she served four years as assisting bishop of the Diocese of Washington, DC and

Whereas, over the years she has been a companion along the way and is considered a cherished colleague and dear friend to many in the House,

Be it resolved, that on this occasion of the 25th anniversary of the consecration of Barbara C. Harris, the members of the House of Bishops of the Episcopal Church acknowledge and celebrate her witness among us, giving thanks that she has been a valiant seeker after truth, liberty, and justice, and rejoicing that all along this Christian journey she has walked closely with her savior.

2014